Cooking with Nora

COOKING WITH

Seasonal Menus from
Restaurant Nora

*Healthy, Light, Balanced and Simple Food
with Organic Ingredients*

by Nora Pouillon

Photography by Koji Hayashi

Foreward by Ben Bradlee and Sally Quinn

A Judd Publishing Book

Park Lane Press
New York ❖ *New Jersey*

Dedicated to Larry Stern and Maya Miller

who first saw my potential
and allowed a dream to become reality

Additional photography ©1996
Gozen Koshida: Pages 5 (lower left), 7, 8, 62-63, 103, 140, 150-151, 168, 187, 204 and back cover.
Paul Fetters: Front cover and cover author photograph.

Book design by Kathy Klingaman
Production and design assistance by Nancy Judd and Elizabeth Reeder

This 1996 edition is published by Park Lane Press, a division of Random House Value Publishing, Inc., 40 Englehard Avenue, Avenel, New Jersey 07001, by arrangement with Judd Publishing, Inc., 3301 N. Albemarle Street, Arlington, Virginia 22207 Published in the Japanese language by Shibata Publishing Company under the editorial direction of Hiromi Hayashi with the title *Nora Cooking in a Healthy Way.*

Random House
New York ❖ Toronto ❖ London ❖ Sydney ❖ Auckland

Printed and bound in the United States of America
Library of Congress Cataloging-in-Publication Data

Pouillon, Nora.
Cooking with Nora : seasonal menus from Restaurant Nora : healthy, light, balanced, and simple food with organic ingredients / by Nora Pouillon.
          p.   cm.
Includes index.
ISBN 0-517-20010-4
1. Cookery (Natural foods) 2. Restaurant Nora. I. Title.
TX741.P68   1996   95-25599
641.5'63—dc20   CIP

8 7 6 5 4 3 2 1

CONTENTS

FOREWORD

One of the seediest, spookiest joints in Washington's Dupont Circle area during the '60s and '70s was a dingy greasy spoon at Florida Avenue and R Street, known phonetically as Boshko's. Sometimes it was a bar, sometimes, a delicatessen, and briefly, a restaurant. But if you didn't like overdone Yugoslavian meatballs, you had to be really hungry or full of Slivovitz to actually eat there.

There really was a "Bosko," a mysterious, brooding hulk of a man from Montenegro in Yugoslavia, named Bosco Milinic, who dispensed booze, cold cuts, milk, butter, and eggs in a kind of surly silence. The clientele consisted of people who looked and acted just like Bosco, or more friendly neighborhood types. Generally in their 30's, two or three rungs up the ladder from hippies, en route to establishment digs in Georgetown, Cleveland Park, or the burbs. Rumor had it that FBI agents would drop by to have a word with Bosco, every so often. No details offered, or received.

Bosco had a long-suffering American wife, Nancy, who slaved behind the counter, while holding part-time jobs as a supermarket bagger and Yellow Cab driver, and raising a small daughter and son.

We lived around the corner on 21st street, next door to Larry Stern, our distinguished *Washington Post* colleague, and the unofficial mayor of our neighborhood. The three of us normally drove to work together a little after nine in the morning, and barring a late-breaking big story, we drove back together about eight, a convenient hour for the first drink of the day, but not a convenient time to start cooking anything worth eating. Mourning the lack of a really good neighborhood bistro was one of our favorite topics of conversation, along with the latest outrage in the White House or on the Hill, and the endlessly interesting details of Stern's love life.

One day, Larry announced that "Nora and two guys" were going to buy Bosco's and open a really good restaurant. "And they need a little money," he added.

"Nora" was Nora Pouillon, a 35-year old Austrian, who ran a cooking school and the restaurant at the Tabard Inn, a funky, friendly old-fashioned hotel on N Street in downtown Washington. "Two guys" were the Damato brothers—Steven who managed the Tabard Inn and doubled as Nora's boyfriend, and Thomas, just back from a Peace Corps tour in Santo Domingo. They did need some money, but not much. They had already raised most of it. We were temporarily flush from some book project, and we chipped in modestly. Just before Christmas 1978, the walls came tumbling down, and out of the brick dust emerged the great institution that is Nora's Restaurant today—gourmet food, elegantly prepared, made only from the healthiest, organically grown meat and vegetables, produced by local growers.

For those of you who equate "organic" with tasteless brown rice, bean sprouts, or tofu, forget it. This is tasty and tasteful food, cooked with a magic touch.

Ben Bradlee and Sally Quinn

INTRODUCTION

Because I was born in Vienna, it is logical to think that my family—like most Austrians in the 1940's—ate lots of fried foods, overcooked vegetables, and pastries with "Schlag" (whipped cream). This was not the case in our house! My father and mother had precise ideas about the upbringing of their daughters, ideas that were considered eccentric and even a bit crazy. I was raised on fresh and simply prepared foods, foods grown locally and eaten soon after harvest. Because nothing was sprayed or injected with drugs or other chemicals, little preparation was required and no heavy sauces were necessary to doctor the flavor. When cherries were juicy and ripe is when we ate them, sometimes straight from the trees.

To further our appreciation for what my parents considered fine food, they enrolled my sisters and me in the Lycée Français de Vienne, a half-boarding school where lunch was a sit-down, four-course meal of aromatic soups, crisp vegetables, lovely roasts, and fresh fish. I still remember these meals.

I feel fortunate to have grown up in such a home, and I never felt deprived. Occasionally, my mother served "Wiener schnitzel" or chocolate torte. But such rich dishes were balanced by simpler meals.

I now realize that my parents' ideas, ideas considered bizarre by our Viennese neighbors, were simply ahead of their time. Today, organic, seasonal ingredients prepared in a simple, healthful manner are in step with how many people want to eat. This sort of cooking is the foundation of Restaurant Nora, where I have been chef for fourteen years.

In 1979 when Restaurant Nora opened, buying locally grown, chemical- and preservative-free foods wasn't easy. There were only three organic farmers in the area and two organic distributors. One farmer raised our beef, two others tended vegetables and herbs, and the distributors provided us with limited amounts of organic foods from other regions. As the interest in healthful food has grown, my resources have expanded. Now I work with more than a dozen organic farmers and three distributors. You will learn more about some of these farmers later in the book.

I believe organic and sustainable agriculture to be an important way to provide a healthy, safe environment for the present and future generations. The use of chemical pesticides and fertilizers in conventional farming has contaminated our groundwater, lakes, and streams.

My commitment to quality remains constant, yet the menus at Restaurant Nora change daily and reflect the diversity of ethnic traditions throughout America and abroad. But no matter what its origin, I use organic ingredients and prepare all my food in a healthful way. Sauces are made with olive oil or canola oil instead of high-cholesterol butter or cream, and I cut fat by grilling, sautéing, or steaming food instead of frying it.

Over the years, first as a home cook, later as a caterer, and today as a chef, I have been asked how I prepare my food and why it tastes so good. People want recipes and techniques for healthful dining. I will tell you—the key to success with any recipe is to find the freshest organic ingredients. When food tastes good, you won't need to eat as much to feel satisfied. And the preparations can be simpler, allowing the cook to share more time with family and friends. Dining healthfully is also about balance and making wise choices, be it in a restaurant or at home. If you really crave a bacon and cheese omelet, eat one! Just weigh it against what else you eat that day or week.

The other aspect of my parents' legacy is the belief that the way we eat and the way we live are intertwined. My sisters and I grew up skiing and hiking. In the summer my mother would take us to France or to Italian beaches where we enjoyed the refreshing ocean air. Today, I firmly believe that some form of daily exercise, even a 20-minute walk, is an important way to balance the effects of what you consume. Increasing your metabolism helps to burn calories and keep you energetic.

For 16 years, I have worked to provide my customers with the best food available, prepared in the best way for both health and enjoyment. Happily, restaurant reviewers consistently include Restaurant Nora on their lists of the best places to eat in the United States. The success of Nora inspired me to open a second restaurant in 1986. We named it City Cafe, offering the same high quality food with a more casual, bistro-style menu and environment.

Recently I have become enchanted with the cuisines of Asia—the simple, healthful preparations and the bold, exciting flavors. That is why last year, I decided to recreate the City Cafe space as the exotic and seductive Asia Nora. Now the menu features my interpretations of dishes from the different Asian cuisines—a blend of East and West—what some call fusion cuisine. The response to Asia Nora has been overwhelming—guests and critics love it!

The menus that follow have been taken from Restaurant Nora.

Nora Pouillon
September 1995
Washington, D.C.

HOW TO USE THIS BOOK

This book is organized into seasons because at Restaurant Nora, what we buy and serve is largely determined by the time of year. Root vegetables are appropriate to chilly winter evenings, and pencil-thin asparagus to the early days of spring.

Within each season, you will find five, four-course menus complete with wine suggestions and nutritional information. I have also added recipes for four vegetarian dishes, plus vegetarian menu ideas. While a four-course meal is perfect for special occasions, one or two courses—an appetizer and dessert, or maybe salad and main course—are more suited to daily dining. But don't be limited to my suggestions! Combine recipes from different menus to develop many other meals.

Within each menu, the recipes are ordered as they would be prepared in the restaurant. "Mise en place" this is called, "putting everything in place." Within a single course, recipes are listed in the order they should be cooked. The side dishes and sauces are executed first, then the "pièce de résistance" or the main dish, so that the whole meal is finished at the same time. To learn this organizational step is important to the success of both family meals and fancy dinner parties.

Unless otherwise stated, all recipes are calculated for four servings.

I have also included symbols for all recipes that can be made a day ahead. ✳ is the symbol for dishes that can be prepared a day ahead. ❖ is the symbol for dishes that should be prepared a day ahead.

How food looks on a plate is important. To help make dishes aesthetically pleasing, each recipe includes a section called "Assembly". I have included other tips, comments, and stories in a section called "Nora's Note." At the restaurant, for example, we always serve hot food on warmed plates and cold food on room temperature plates.

The recipes in this book, like the food at Restaurant Nora, depend on high-quality, healthy ingredients. For best results, I recommend using organic meat, poultry, and vegetables bought either from markets that specialize in such foods or from local organic farmers. In addition to being healthier to eat, I find food raised organically superior in flavor to that which is commercially produced.

My travels have led me to appreciate the staples of other cultures, and I often use Asian ingredients, such as tamari, tahini, garam masala, ginger, or chilies. If you have trouble finding these at your local market, try a health food or specialty store.

EQUIPMENT

Everyone's kitchen is different, but certain pieces of equipment make food preparation both faster and simpler. To me, a basic kitchen includes:

- four sharp knives—a serrated knife, and one each for slicing, chopping, and paring
- a cutting board
- measuring cups and spoons
- a pepper mill
- non-stick sauté pans or seasoned, cast-iron skillets
- stainless steel or ceramic pots and pans
- a collapsible vegetable steamer
- a salad spinner
- a blender or food processor
- a hand or electric mixer or whip
- an ice cream maker, either electric or hand-cranked
- a roller-type pasta machine
- a broiler or a grill—small, stovetop grills work perfectly and are easy to use and clean

It is important that saucepans and pots, except for cast-iron skillets, be non-reactive stainless steel or ceramic to prevent the chemical changes that can occur with acidic ingredients like citrus juices, wine, vinegar, or tomatoes. Cooking with aluminum can alter flavors, and there remains concern that traces of aluminum leached into foods may be unhealthy.

FATS

Oil: Olive oil is my favorite oil. It is a healthful, monounsaturated fat that receives little processing, especially cold-pressed "extra virgin" and "virgin" olive oils. There is a wide range of olive oil flavors and qualities. When sautéing, choose a mild, light-colored, "virgin" olive oil. For dressings, pasta dishes, and relishes, where the oil's flavor is important, select a darker, more flavorful "extra virgin" olive oil. If you are trying to reduce your fat intake, I recommend the new olive oil sprays. For Asian dishes requiring a more neutral flavor, I use canola oil, another monounsaturated oil. Sometimes I mix canola oil with small amounts of sesame oil to use in marinades, vinaigrettes, and stir fry sauces. All of these oils can be found in most supermarkets and health food stores.

Butter: I use butter only when baking. Be sure it is unsalted.

Cheese: I use a lot of goat cheese. Though high in fat, I love its flavor and find it easier to digest than other cheeses. If you are on a low-fat diet, substitute low-fat ricotta, which has half the calories of goat cheese, or make your own low-fat yogurt cheese by draining low-fat yogurt in a cheesecloth-lined colander overnight. Cut more fat by using high-quality products like Parmigiano-Reggiano or fresh mozzarella. Because of their superior flavor, you can use less.

Seasonings

Herbs And Spices: An herb garden grows in front of Restaurant Nora—a good thing, too, because I use fresh herbs by the handful: basil, cilantro, rosemary, thyme, oregano, chives, and flat leaf parsley (more flavorful and higher in iron than curly parsley). For dried herbs and spices, I prefer blends; they are used up faster, and therefore taste fresher. Some favorites are bouquet garni, herbes de Provence, raz el hanout, curry, quatre épices, and garam masala. Look for these at ethnic markets or specialty food stores. (Better yet, do it yourself. I have provided recipes to blend your own.)

Salt: I use sea salt because it has fewer chemical additives than table salt, is less processed, and has more flavor. I also use a lot of tamari sauce because it is both salty and flavorful and contains no wheat products. Soy sauce makes a fine substitute. If you are on a low-sodium diet, use light or low-sodium tamari or soy.

Pepper: I use only black pepper, and my favorite is Telicherry. I like its strong flavor. I buy whole peppercorns and grind them with a pepper mill. When pepper is freshly ground, it has much more flavor than packaged ground pepper. At the restaurant, I grind a half-cup every morning in a blender. It is much easier than using a small hand mill. Fresh and dried chili peppers are also important for adding heat and flavor, but use caution when working with them. Be careful not to touch your eyes, and be sure to wash your hands after handling them.

Sugar: I never use sugar substitutes. I don't think they have been proven safe, and there is even some evidence that they increase food cravings. For a low-calorie diet, decrease sugar intake and substitute vanilla and fruit juices for a sweet flavor. Raw honey and blackstrap molasses are other sources of sweetness.

Vinegar: Balsamic is my favorite because it is mellow and has lots of flavor. You only need to add a little oil to make a delicious and simple dressing. For milder flavored vinegars, try sherry, rice, or organic apple cider vinegars.

Liquids

Stocks: Stocks can be time-consuming for the home cook. At the restaurant, we make veal and chicken stock three times a week in an enormous steam kettle. For home use, I suggest buying unsalted chicken (or vegetable) stock from a health food store and enriching it by simmering the broth with additional bones (or aromatic vegetables).

Water: Not only do I drink a lot of water, I use a lot of it in my cooking. I recommend filtered or bottled water because many city waters contain chemical additives. Restaurant Nora has a sophisticated filtering system to ensure that our water is the purest possible.

Alcohol: A bottle of unpasteurized beer or a glass of wine complements a meal and, for me, is part of healthy eating and living. The key is moderation. These days, there are many organic wines to choose from that will complement all variety of healthy foods.

NUTRITIONAL INFORMATION

In this book, most recipes are created for four servings. The nutritional information provided with each recipe is for one serving. Caloric content is divided into proteins, carbohydrates, and fats listed in grams (g) and calories (cal).

Protein is required for growth and maintenance of all tissues. Fifteen to twenty percent of total daily calories should come from protein. It is recommended that for each pound of ideal body weight, an adult should take in 0.36 grams of protein. Protein provides 4 calories per gram.

Carbohydrates are the body's main source of energy. Fifty-five to sixty-eight percent of total daily calories should come from carbohydrates. The most nutritious source of carbohydrates are whole grains, vegetables, and fruits. Carbohydrates provide 4 calories per gram.

Fats are an energy source, supply essential fatty acids, carry fat-soluble Vitamin A, D, E, and K, and provide satiety. No more than 30 percent of daily calories should come from fat, with no more than 10 percent from saturated fats, up to 10 percent from polyunsaturated, and the balance from monosaturated fats. Fats provide 9 calories per gram.

Sodium maintains the body's fluid balance, and plays a major role in nervous system health. A level of 1,100-3,300 milligrams of sodium per day is considered safe for the average healthy adult.

Cholesterol is only found in animal products, including dairy foods, whole eggs, poultry, fish, and meat. It is recommended that daily intake not exceed 300 milligrams.

Dietary fiber is essential to good health. The National Cancer Institute suggests that adults consume at least 20-30 grams per day.

Nora and I have chosen this way of nutrient listing for the ease of finding the percentage of the calories.

To further aid in your nutritional understanding, Nora and I have provided information about an added nutrient if a recipe meets a significant percent of that nutrient's daily requirement. Daily requirements have been created by the Food and Drug Administration and the US Department of Agriculture, to allow individuals to make more healthful choices. The nutrients we have chosen to focus on are Vitamin A, Vitamin C, calcium, and iron.

Lauren R. Braun, Registered Dietitian, L.D.
Owner of Nutitional Lifestyle Designs

SPRING

SPRING MENU I

Asparagus Soup with Comfrey Flowers and Light Cream

Natural Shrimp and Virginia Morel Mushroom Risotto with Saffron, Spinach,
and English Peas

Baby Head Lettuce and Radicchio with Brie, Spicy Walnuts,
and Sherry Vinaigrette

Strawberries with Bittersweet Chocolate Dipping Sauce

WINE SELECTIONS

A crisp, dry, medium bodied Italian white, such as a Pinot Grigio or a Vernaccia, is perfect for the risotto.

Pinot Grigio 1991 Pighin

Vernaccia di San Gimignano 1991 Teruzzi and Puthod

Asparagus Soup with
Comfrey Flowers and Light Cream*

1 tablespoon canola oil
1 large onion, chopped
2 ribs celery, including greens, chopped
½ pound asparagus, cut into 1-inch pieces
2 tablespoons rice
1 cup milk
1 cup water
1 ounce spinach, stemmed

1 tablespoon lemon juice
Pinch nutmeg
Pinch cayenne
Sea salt
4 teaspoons light whipped cream or crème
    fraîche, for garnish
Comfrey or chive blossoms or other edible
    flowers for garnish

Heat the oil in a medium saucepan and sauté the onion for 5 minutes, or until the onion is soft and clear. Add the celery, asparagus, and rice and stir until coated with oil. Add the milk and the water and bring to a boil. Reduce the heat, cover, and simmer for about 20 minutes or until the asparagus and celery are soft.

Let cool. Add the spinach, lemon juice, and nutmeg. Purée in a blender until smooth. Strain through a colander to remove the asparagus fiber, pushing the liquid through with a rubber spatula. Season to taste with salt and cayenne.

Assembly: Reheat the soup and pour into individual soup bowls. Garnish with a dollop of light whipping cream and comfrey blossoms or other edible flowers.

ASPARAGUS SOUP
Calories 105;   Protein 5 g/19 cal;   Carbohydrates 12 g/48 cal;
Fat 4 g/38 cal;   (Saturated Fat .4 g/4 cal);   Cholesterol 1 mg;
Sodium 56 mg;   Fiber 2 g;   Calcium 14% of Daily Value

Be sure to add spices such as cayenne after you have puréed a soup or a sauce in the blender because the taste of a spice intensifies when it is blended, making it difficult to judge how much to add.

At the restaurant we generally use asparagus stems to make this soup. It is a great way to use them. I add spinach to the soup for color.

Adding milk and rice makes a creamy vegetable soup without the calories.

Natural Shrimp and Virginia Morel Mushroom Risotto with Saffron, Spinach, and English Peas

Risotto *

This is how we prepare risotto in the restaurant so we can be ready to produce a finished dish once the order comes. A great time-saver for entertaining, you can finish this precooked risotto in just a few minutes.

Small quantities of leftover risotto make a good stuffing for chicken breast or can be mixed with sautéed wild mushrooms, formed into patties, and sautéed. A wild mushroom risotto cake served with a salad makes a nice lunch or supper.

2 tablespoons olive oil
4 tablespoons minced shallots
2 tablespoons minced garlic
1 1/2 cups (1 pound) arborio rice, available at specialty stores

2 cups white wine, a mix of shrimp stock and white wine, or water
1/2 teaspoon saffron threads
Sea salt and freshly ground pepper

Heat the oil in a deep sauté pan, add the shallots, and sauté for 4 minutes or until soft and clear. Add the garlic, sauté 1 minute, add the rice and, stirring to coat, sauté until the rice is translucent—about 1 minute. Add 1 cup of the wine, stock, and/or water, and the saffron. Season to taste with salt and pepper.

Bring to a boil, reduce the heat, and simmer for 5 – 8 minutes, stirring frequently, until the liquid is absorbed.

Add the remaining cup of liquid and cook, stirring frequently, for about 12 minutes or until rice is al dente.

Remove from the heat and spread the rice onto a baking sheet. Allow to cool. The recipe can be made ahead to this point.

*¹/₂ pound morel mushrooms, washed and
  dried*
2 tablespoons olive oil
2 tablespoons minced garlic
1 pound shrimp, shelled and deveined
Sea salt and freshly ground pepper

4 cups precooked risotto
1 cup green peas, shelled
4 ounces spinach, stemmed and cut in julienne
1 — 1¹/₂ cups water or shrimp stock
Chives for garnish (optional)

You can improve this risotto by using shrimp stock made with the shells. Put the shells in a non-reactive saucepan with some water, white wine, a carrot, a celery rib, bay leaf, parsley, salt and pepper. Bring to a boil, reduce the heat, and simmer 20 minutes. Strain the stock through a fine sieve.

If the morels are larger than 2½ inches, cut them into ½-inch slices.

Heat the olive oil in a large, deep, sauté pan, add the garlic, and stir for 1 minute. Add the shrimp and morels, stir, season to taste with salt and pepper, and sauté for about 2 minutes. Add the precooked risotto, peas, spinach, and as much water or stock as necessary to cook the vegetables and reheat the risotto. Stir to combine, bring to a boil, and cook until the risotto develops the consistency of a liquid creamy cereal.

ASSEMBLY: Serve the risotto in 4 large soup plates. Garnish with the chives.

Try making this risotto with other kinds of mushrooms. If fresh mushrooms are unavailable, dried morels, porcinis, or boletus are good substitutes. Soak them in warm water for 30 minutes until soft, drain, and proceed as if they were fresh. Keep the liquid for cooking the rice, but strain it through a fine sieve.

RISOTTO
Calories 232;   Protein 5 g/21 cal;   Carbohydrates 26 g/105 cal;
Fat 12 g/106 cal;   (Saturated Fat 2 g/16 cal);   Cholesterol 0 mg;
Sodium 6 mg;   Fiber 3 g;   Iron 45% of Daily Value

SHRIMP AND VEGETABLES
Calories 191;   Protein 26 g/105 cal;   Carbohydrates 9 g/34 cal;
Fat 6 g/52 cal;   (Saturated Fat 1 g/8 cal);   Cholesterol 172 mg;
Sodium 195 mg;   Fiber 3 g;   Iron 33% of Daily Value

BABY HEAD LETTUCE AND RADICCHIO SALAD WITH BRIE, SPICY WALNUTS, AND SHERRY VINAIGRETTE

SHERRY VINAIGRETTE *

The sherry vinaigrette is a good marinade for pork chops or grilled mushrooms. It is also a delicious dressing for a Belgian endive, mâche, apple, and walnut salad or a chicken salad with pears, pecans, and frisée lettuce.

Sea salt and freshly ground black pepper
1 tablespoon sherry vinegar

3 tablespoons extra-virgin olive oil

Mix the salt, pepper, and sherry vinegar in a small bowl until the salt dissolves. Add the olive oil slowly, while whisking with a fork.

SPICY WALNUTS ✳

Use ¼ cup for the salad, store the rest in an
    airtight container
2 teaspoons canola oil
1 egg white
½ teaspoon salt

⅛ teaspoon cayenne
¼ teaspoon powdered ginger
1½ cups walnuts, preferably English walnut
    halves

Preheat the oven to 350° F.

    Oil a small, 8 x 10-inch, baking dish with 1 teaspoon of the oil. Mix the egg
white, remaining oil, salt, cayenne, and ginger together in a medium bowl. Add
the walnuts and stir to coat. Spread them out on the oiled baking sheet and bake
for 15 – 20 minutes, stirring from time to time, or until toasted and fragrant.
Allow to cool.

I like this low-fat way of preparing spicy nuts with egg whites rather than deep frying. Use this same technique to prepare other nuts such as pecans, cashews, or peanuts.

This recipe doesn't work with a small quantity of nuts. I suggest you make more and store the remaining nuts in an airtight container for another use.

BABY HEAD LETTUCES, RADICCHIO, AND BRIE

½ pound baby lettuces, washed and spun dry
1 head radicchio, washed, spun dry, and torn
    into pieces

¼ pound Brie, cut into 16 pieces
Sherry vinaigrette

ASSEMBLY: Toss the lettuces and radicchio in the sherry vinaigrette. Divide onto
4 large salad plates. Top each with 4 pieces of Brie and a sprinkling of spicy walnuts.

SHERRY VINAIGRETTE
Calories 90;　Protein 0 g/0 cal;　Carbohydrates .25 g/1 cal;
Fat 10 g/89 cal;　(Saturated Fat 1 g/13 cal);　Cholesterol 0 mg;
Sodium 53 mg;　Fiber 0 g

SALAD OF BABY HEAD LETTUCES,
RADICCHIO AND BRIE
Calories 107;　Protein 9 g/34 cal;　Carbohydrates 2 g/6 cal;
Fat 7 g/67 cal;　(Saturated Fat 1 g/10 cal);　Cholesterol 28 mg;
Sodium 190 mg;　Fiber 2 g;　Vitamin A 61% of Daily Value

SPICY WALNUTS
Calories 72;　Protein 3 g/11 cal;　Carbohydrates 1 g/5 cal;
Fat 6 g/56 cal;　(Saturated Fat .4 g/4 cal);　Cholesterol 0 mg;
Sodium 280 mg;　Fiber 1 g;　Iron 1% of Daily Value

Vary this salad by using Stilton or goat cheese instead of Brie and pecans or almonds instead of walnuts.

Austin, the farmer at Stonebridge Farm, grows beautiful baby lettuces for us. One head is just perfect for one serving. They have wonderful names such as French Batavia, Little Gems, and Red Ruby.

STRAWBERRIES WITH BITTERSWEET CHOCOLATE DIPPING SAUCE*

I adapted this dessert from a traditional Swiss fondue. My customers love it, especially when local strawberries are in season. In the winter, I sometimes serve it with orange and clementine sections or banana pieces to dip in the chocolate sauce.

6 ounces good quality bittersweet chocolate, Belgian or French
3 tablespoons heavy cream
3 tablespoons Grand Marnier

1½ – 2 pints large ripe strawberries, washed, and drained
Fresh mint for garnish

Put the chocolate, the cream, and the Grand Marnier in a double boiler. Melt over simmering water, stirring from time to time.

ASSEMBLY: Pour the warm chocolate sauce into four 3-inch, ceramic ramekins. Place each in the center of a dinner plate and surround them with strawberries. Garnish with mint.

STRAWBERRIES WITH BITTERSWEET
CHOCOLATE DIPPING SAUCE
Calories 337;   Protein 6 g/23 cal;   Carbohydrates 26 g/105 cal;
Fat 23 g/209 cal;   (Saturated Fat 16 g/143 cal);   Cholesterol 15 mg;
Sodium 7 mg;   Fiber 10 g;   Iron 22% of Daily Value

SPRING MENU II

Sautéed Shad Roe with Mustard Sauce, Red Cabbage Salad, and Grilled Onions

Veal Scaloppine with Morel Mushroom Sauce, Pappardelle Pasta,
and Baby Turnips with their Greens

Watercress and Red Mustard Greens with Red Bell Peppers and Ginger-Tamari Dressing

Old Fashioned Carrot Cake with Light Whipped Cream

WINE SELECTIONS

*A young, soft Burgundy is a good match for young meat. The delicate fruit flavor of a
Santennay or a Beaune Cent Vignes would not overpower the fine flavor of veal.*

Santennay Clos de Malte 1989 Louis Jadot

Beaune Cent Vignes 1990 Albert Morot

SAUTÉED SHAD ROE WITH MUSTARD SAUCE, RED CABBAGE SALAD, AND GRILLED ONIONS

RED CABBAGE SALAD ✳

1 small red cabbage, about ³/₄ – 1 pound

4 tablespoons red wine or water

2 tablespoons red wine vinegar

2 teaspoons caraway seeds

1 tablespoon canola oil

¹/₂ teaspoon sea salt

1 teaspoon freshly ground black pepper

Slice the cabbage as thinly as possible, by hand or in a food processor. Mix the red wine, vinegar, caraway seeds, canola oil, and salt and pepper to taste in a large bowl. Add the cabbage and toss. Allow to marinate for at least 20 minutes before serving.

GRILLED SPRING ONIONS

2 teaspoons olive oil

2 teaspoons tamari

Freshly ground black pepper

8 large green onions, trimmed

Preheat the grill or the broiler.

Mix the olive oil, tamari, and black pepper in a small bowl. Pour onto a flat plate and turn the onions in the sauce until well coated. Grill or broil the onions about 2 – 5 minutes per side or until brown and softened.

In the winter, I add some chopped onions to this cabbage salad and cook it for about a half hour. It makes a great vegetable to serve with grilled pork chops and sautéed apples. For a sauce, use the same mustard sauce I serve with the shad roe.

I like grilled vegetables. They are tasty as an appetizer, with balsamic vinaigrette or hummus, or as a vegetable, with grilled meat or fish. Carrots lightly steamed, brushed with a marinade, and then grilled, are a good choice in the winter when fewer colorful vegetables are available.

Shad is from the herring family and is therefore a fatty fish, unfortunately high in cholesterol.

The shad season lasts about four months, from February to May. The anadromous shad "runs" from Florida to Maine to spawn in the rivers where it hatched. Native Americans and early settlers swarmed to the riverbanks each spring to feast on shad and its roe, as they did in the fall for eels.

3 tablespoons olive oil
4 shallots, sliced
4 cloves garlic, sliced
1 tablespoon tamari
½ cup veal or chicken stock or water
1 teaspoon balsamic vinegar
1½ tablespoons Dijon mustard

5 sage leaves or 1 teaspoon thyme leaves

2 sets shad roe, 4 – 6 ounces each, cut into halves
Sea salt
Freshly ground black pepper
Marigold flowers for garnish

Heat 2 tablespoons of the olive oil in a small sauté pan and sauté the shallot and garlic for 3 – 4 minutes or until soft. Pour this mixture in a blender and add tamari, stock or water, vinegar, mustard, and sage or thyme leaves. Purée until smooth.

Soak the shad roe in ice cold water for a few minutes. Remove from the water and dry on paper towels.

Prick the skin of the roe with a fork or the tip of a sharp knife to prevent it from bursting while cooking or gently parboil them in water for about 5 minutes to firm them before sautéing.

Heat the remaining olive oil in a large sauté pan. Be careful while sautéing— despite your precautions, the roe can burst and spatter you with tiny eggs. Sauté the roe over low heat for 6 – 8 minutes on each side if raw, less if you have parboiled them. They should be browned and cooked through. Season the roe to taste with salt and pepper.

ASSEMBLY: Put a shad roe on each plate. Pour some of the mustard sauce over and around each roe. Put a spoonful of the cabbage salad in the center, add the grilled green onions, and garnish with marigold flowers.

RED CABBAGE SALAD
Calories 83; Protein 2 g/9 cal; Carbohydrates 10 g/39 cal;
Fat 4 g/35 cal; (Saturated Fat .3 g/3 cal); Cholesterol 0 mg;
Sodium 123 mg; Fiber 3 g; Vitamin C 135% of Daily Value

GRILLED SPRING ONIONS
Calories 31; Protein 1 g/4 cal; Carbohydrates 2 g/9 cal;
Fat 2 g/18 cal; (Saturated Fat .3 g/3 cal); Cholesterol 0 mg;
Sodium 169 mg; Fiber 1 g; Vitamin C 26% of Daily Value

SHAD ROE WITH MUSTARD SAUCE
Calories 310; Protein 44 g/176 cal; Carbohydrates 4 g/16 cal;
Fat 13 g/117 cal; (Saturated Fat 1.5 g/13.5 cal); Cholesterol 80 mg;
Sodium 450 mg; Fiber 0 g; Iron 15% of Daily Value

Veal Scaloppine with Morel Mushroom Sauce, Pappardelle Pasta, and Baby Turnips with their Greens

Pappardelle Pasta *

You will need a pasta machine or a source for fresh pasta

1¹/₂ cups all-purpose flour
³/₄ cup semolina flour

Pinch saffron powder or turmeric (optional)
1 teaspoon salt
3 eggs
1 teaspoon olive oil

Put the flours, saffron or turmeric, and salt in the bowl of a food processor and pulse to combine. Add the eggs and olive oil and process the dough for about 30 seconds or until it forms a ball. If the dough is too wet or too dry and does not form a ball, add additional flour or water, teaspoon by teaspoon, while the machine is running, processing the dough until it has the desired consistency.

Cut the dough into 8 pieces, flatten each into an oval, and dust with flour. Set the rollers of the pasta machine at the widest setting. Run each portion of dough through 10 times, folding and turning it each time. This is the kneading step.

Close the roller setting one notch and run one piece of dough through, flouring the dough or rollers if necessary.

Keep narrowing the roller settings, notch by notch, and pass the dough through, gradually stretching it until it is about ¹/₁₆ of an inch for pappardelle.

Lay the pasta sheets on a lightly floured surface. Do not overlap. Allow them to dry for 5 minutes or until the dough loses enough moistness to separate easily when folded and cut.

Roll each pasta sheet until it forms a short rectangular roll about 3-inches wide. Cut the pappardelle noodles by hand, about ¾ – 1-inch wide. Unfold the noodles and spread them out to dry for 5 minutes before cooking.

Bring a large pot of water to a boil and add ¹/₂ tablespoon olive oil. Just before serving, cook the pasta for 3 minutes or until al dente. Drain, season to taste with salt and pepper, and add a few drops of olive oil to prevent the noodles from sticking together.

I like to use semolina flour in my pasta dough because it makes a firmer pasta with a nice tooth and is easier to cook al dente. A pinch of saffron powder or turmeric added to the flour gives the dough a nice yellow color.

This recipe is the standard for all types of pasta: fettuccine, spaghetti, and lasagna. If you want colorful, flavored pasta such as basil, spinach, or beet, add 4 tablespoons puréed basil, cooked puréed spinach, or beet to the dough, use 2 eggs instead of 3, and increase the amount of flour until you get the right consistency. For other flavored pastas, add dried spices such as black pepper, chili powder, or ground cumin to the dough.

Baby Turnips and Their Greens

8 – 12 baby turnips (about 1 pound) washed, with greens attached

1 teaspoon olive oil
Sea salt and freshly ground black pepper

Cut an "X" on the base of the turnips, about ¹/₂-inch deep, to speed the cooking.

In the spring, our farmers in Pennsylvania bring us beautiful baby turnips and beets, so fresh, they don't need peeling. Turnips are from the cabbage family and many people boil

Using a collapsible steamer, steam the turnips in a medium saucepan for 5 to 10 minutes, depending on the size of the turnips. Remove the turnips from the saucepan and toss them with the olive oil, and salt and pepper to taste.

MOREL MUSHROOM SAUCE *

½ pound morel mushrooms, washed, drained, and stems trimmed
2 tablespoons olive oil
¼ cup minced shallots
2 tablespoons minced garlic
½ cup sherry or white wine

½ cup veal stock or water with ½ bouillon cube
Sea salt and freshly ground black pepper
2 tablespoons mixed fresh herbs such as flat leaf parsley, sage, and thyme

If the morels are larger than 2-inches, cut into 1-inch slices. Heat the olive oil in a medium sauté pan and sauté the shallots for 4 minutes. Add the garlic, and sauté 2 minutes. Add the morels and sauté 2 more minutes, stirring. Add the sherry or wine and stock or water and bouillon. Bring to a boil and cook until sauce is reduced by half. Remove from heat. Season to taste with salt and pepper and the fresh herbs.

16 — 20 veal scaloppine, about 1 pound cut from the leg, ¼-inch thick

*Sea salt and freshly ground black pepper
3 — 4 tablespoons olive oil*

Season the scaloppine with salt and pepper. Heat 1 tablespoon of olive oil in a large sauté pan until very hot. Put as many veal scaloppine in the pan as can fit in one layer without touching. Sauté 1 — 2 minutes on each side or until brown. Sauté the remaining scaloppine in batches, using the remaining oil as necessary, until all are completed. Cover the cooked scaloppine with aluminum foil to keep warm while preparing the rest of the dish.

ASSEMBLY: Put 4 — 5 veal scaloppine on each of 4 large dinner plates and spoon some morel mushroom sauce over them. Add a serving of the pappardelle pasta to each plate and the steamed turnips with their greens. Garnish with fresh herbs.

I never pound my veal. Instead, I slice it as thin as possible. The veal we use at Nora's is organically raised and is a little tougher than what is generally available, but juicier. Veal scaloppine cooks so quickly that it is very important to start with a hot pan. Otherwise you risk overcooking or steaming the veal and not getting a nice brown color.

PAPPARADELLE PASTA
Calories 171;   Protein 7 g/27 cal;   Carbohydrates 30 g/118 cal;
Fat 3 g/25 cal;   (Saturated Fat .6 g/6 cal);   Cholesterol 80 mg;
Sodium 157 mg;   Fiber 0 g;   Iron 14% of Daily Value

BABY TURNIPS
Calories 36;   Protein 1 g/3 cal;   Carbohydrates 6 g/23 cal;
Fat 1 g/10 cal;   (Saturated Fat 1 g/7 cal);   Cholesterol 0 mg;
Sodium 9 mg;   Fiber 1 g;   Calcium 5% of Daily Value

MOREL SAUCE
Calories 67;   Protein 2 g/7 cal;   Carbohydrates 7 g/27 cal;
Fat 4 g/33 cal;   (Saturated Fat .5 g/5 cal);   Cholesterol 0 mg;
Sodium 8 mg;   Fiber 1 g;   Iron 9% of Daily Value

VEAL SCALOPPINE
Calories 224;   Protein 32 g/128 cal;   Carbohydrates .25 g/1 cal;
Fat 10 g/95 cal;   (Saturated Fat 2 g/21 cal);   Cholesterol 117 mg;
Sodium 77 mg;   Fiber 0 g;   Iron 7% of Daily Value

WATERCRESS AND RED MUSTARD GREENS SALAD WITH RED BELL PEPPERS AND GINGER-TAMARI DRESSING

GINGER-TAMARI DRESSING

2 small garlic cloves

½-inch piece ginger, peeled and sliced across the long fibers

8 sprigs cilantro

4 small green onions, trimmed and coarsely chopped

1 tablespoon water

1 tablespoon rice wine vinegar

1 tablespoon tamari

1 tablespoon sesame oil

2 tablespoons canola oil

Freshly ground black pepper

¾ pound watercress, washed, stems trimmed, and spun dry

¼ pound baby red mustard leaves, tat soi, or spinach, washed, stemmed, and spun dry

1 small red bell pepper, seeded and cut into ¼-inch dice

My German friend, Gudrun, a very adventurous cook, introduced me to this dressing in the early seventies. This dressing can also be used as a marinade for grilled beef or lamb and makes a good sauce for stir-fried beef with watercress, mustard greens, red peppers, and shiitake mushrooms. It also complements a salad of thinly sliced Chinese cabbage or mung bean sprouts.

Put the garlic, ginger, cilantro, green onions, water, vinegar, and tamari into a blender. Process until smooth. Combine the oils and pour them into the blender in a steady stream, while the motor is running. Blend until emulsified. Season to taste with pepper.

ASSEMBLY: Toss the watercress and mustard greens with the dressing. Divide them among 4 luncheon plates. Sprinkle each salad with some diced red pepper.

WATERCRESS AND RED MUSTARD SALAD
WITH RED BELL PEPPERS
Calories 31; Protein 3 g/13 cal; Carbohydrates 4 g/16 cal;
Fat .2 g/2 cal; (Saturated Fat 0 g/0 cal); Cholesterol 0 mg;
Sodium 62 mg; Fiber 2 g; Vitamin A 80% of Daily Value

GINGER-TAMARI DRESSING
Calories 74; Protein 1 g/4 cal; Carbohydrates 3 g/12 cal;
Fat 6 g/58 cal; (Saturated Fat 0 g/0 cal); Cholesterol 0 mg;
Sodium 253 mg; Fiber 0 g; Vitamin C 23% of Daily Value

OLD FASHIONED CARROT CAKE WITH LIGHT WHIPPED CREAM

This cake has no butter or sugar and is very moist. Being from Austria, where cakes are traditionally made with lots of butter, sugar, eggs, and cream, I was pleased to discover that I could make very good tasting cakes with vegetables and oil. This carrot cake is a favorite of Steven's for breakfast and a very popular dessert at Nora's. I often substitute a mixture of ginger, cardamom, and cinnamon for the spices in this recipe.

I prefer to use unfiltered, raw honey when I can get it. Because raw honey is sweeter than regular honey, I use less.

¼ cup canola oil
2 tablespoons bread crumbs
¾ cup whole-wheat flour
¼ cup all-purpose flour
1 teaspoon baking soda
1 teaspoon cinnamon
¼ teaspoon nutmeg
¼ teaspoon allspice
¼ teaspoon cloves
¼ teaspoon sea salt
2 large eggs

⅓ cup buttermilk or ⅓ cup milk soured with
   1 teaspoon lemon juice
¾ cup honey
3 cups grated carrots, about ¾ pounds, peeled,
   shredded, and squeezed dry
½ cup raisins
½ cup walnuts

Light whipped cream (page 53)
Mint or lemon balm for garnish

Preheat oven to 350° F.

Oil a 4 – 6 cup tube pan, bundt pan, or loaf with 1 teaspoon of the oil and dust with the bread crumbs.

Sift the dry ingredients together in a medium bowl: the flours, baking soda, cinnamon, nutmeg, allspice, cloves, and salt. Set aside. Mix the wet ingredients together in a large bowl: the eggs, buttermilk or soured milk, honey, carrots, and remaining oil. Stir in the raisins and nuts. Stir the dry ingredients into the wet ingredients by hand using a large spoon or rubber spatula. Mix well to combine.

Pour the batter into the prepared pan. Bake for 45 – 55 minutes or until a skewer inserted in the middle of the cake comes out clean. Remove the cake from the oven and cool for 10 minutes on a rack. Unmold the cake and allow it to cool on the rack for 30 – 40 minutes before serving.

ASSEMBLY: Slice the cake into generous 2-inch slices. Arrange each piece on a dinner plate and garnish with a spoonful of light whipped cream and a sprig of mint or lemon balm. Serves 12.

CARROT CAKE
Calories 282;   Protein 6 g/22 cal;   Carbohydrates 37 g/146 cal;
Fat 13 g/114 cal;   (Saturated Fat 1 g/13 cal);   Cholesterol 53 mg;
Sodium 188 mg;   Fiber 1 g;   Vitamin A 61% of Daily Value

SPRING MENU III

Salmon Gravlax Napoleon with Shiitakes, Cucumbers, Dandelion,
and Cilantro Vinaigrette

Baby Lettuces with White and Red Radishes and Herb Dressing

Chicken Breast with Couscous-Eggplant-Goat Cheese Stuffing, Moroccan Tomato Sauce, Spaghetti
Squash, Red Chard, and Green Beans

Strawberry Rhubarb Pie with Ginger Ice Cream

WINE SELECTIONS

White wine from France's Rhone valley would be interesting.
The menu has many textures and tastes and needs a wine with a full flavor that will not overpower the food.

Crozes Hermitage 1991 Alain Graillot

Châteauneuf du Pape 1991 Les Cailloux

Salmon Gravlax Napoleon with Shiitakes, Cucumbers, Dandelion, and Cilantro Vinaigrette

❖ SALMON GRAVLAX

Salmon takes 2 days to cure.

*1 – 1½ pounds salmon fillet in one piece,
    with skin*
2 tablespoons sea salt

1½ – 2 tablespoons cracked black pepper
1 teaspoon ground coriander
2 tablespoons sugar
1½ tablespoons brandy
¼ cup chopped cilantro

Carefully remove the small, pin bones from the fillet using tweezers or pliers.

In a small bowl, mix together the salt, pepper, coriander, and sugar. Cut a piece of plastic wrap two times larger than the salmon fillet and lay it on a work surface. Spread the plastic with half of the spice mixture and place the salmon on top, skin side down. Rub the fillet with the remaining spices, sprinkle with brandy, and top with the cilantro. Wrap the plastic wrap tightly around the salmon.

Put the fillet in a non-reactive baking dish and weigh down evenly using a brick or a board weighted with a heavy can.

Refrigerate the salmon while it is curing, turning it once a day. Allow it to cure for 2 days although the thin tail often cures in one day.

✳ CILANTRO VINAIGRETTE

⅓ cup cilantro leaves, tightly packed
2 shallots, peeled
2 cloves of garlic, peeled
1 small green jalapeño chili pepper
1-inch piece of ginger, peeled and sliced

1 tablespoon tamari
1 tablespoon rice wine vinegar
3 tablespoons water
3 tablespoons canola oil

Preheat the oven to 400° F.

Put the garlic and shallots in a small non-reactive baking dish. Dress with 1 teaspoon olive oil and season with salt and pepper. Cover with aluminum foil and roast for 30 – 40 minutes or until soft.

Put the cilantro, shallots, garlic, jalapeño, ginger, tamari, vinegar, water, and oil into a blender. Purée until smooth and emulsified.

When gravlax is on the menu, we keep 3 or 4 salmon fillets curing at all times. I often substitute dill for the cilantro when curing the gravlax.

Salmon is a versatile, popular fish, and I use it a lot. I like salmon from the Pacific Northwest or the Columbia River. I especially like sockeye salmon because it has the reddest color and the smallest flake.

Salmon is rich in Vitamin A, as well as niacin, riboflavin, and other B vitamins.

Make a southwestern pasta with this cilantro vinaigrette by mixing it with some cooked chicken, corn, tomatoes, and thinly sliced red onions.

You can adapt this vinaigrette by substituting basil or dill. Use a basil vinaigrette for a tomato mozzarella salad or grilled chicken. The dill vinaigrette goes well with steamed potatoes and smoked trout or with grilled swordfish.

Layering the salmon gravlax with greens, cucumbers, and shiitakes makes a dramatic presentation which resembles the puff pastry called Napoleon.

If you don't have time to make the gravlax, substitute smoked salmon, but take care not to make the vinaigrette too salty. You can also make gravlax with other fish such as red snapper.

I like cross-cultural cooking— like this Scandinavian recipe with an Asian twist of shiitakes, cilantro, and mizuna (Chinese mustard greens).

1 — 1½ pounds salmon gravlax or smoked salmon
½ teaspoon tamari
½ tablespoon olive oil
⅛ teaspoon freshly ground black pepper

8 — 10 shiitake mushrooms, stems removed
2 small cucumbers, peeled
2 ounces dandelion or mizuna greens, washed and dried

Remove the gravlax from the plastic wrap, pour off the accumulated juices. If too salty, rinse under cold water. Slice in paper thin slices holding the knife at a 45-degree angle.

Preheat the grill or broiler.

Mix the tamari, olive oil, and pepper in a small bowl. Add the shiitake caps and toss to coat evenly. Grill the shiitakes, cap-side-down, or broil on a sheet pan, 2 minutes per side or until soft and cooked through. Cool and slice thinly into julienne strips.

Grate the outside pulp of the cucumbers avoiding the seedy cores. Discard the cores. Drain the cucumber in a colander for 10 — 30 minutes.

ASSEMBLY: Place 1 — 2 slices of gravlax in the center of each of 4 dinner plates. Cover with dandelion or mizuna greens and drizzle with vinaigrette. Add 1 — 2 more slices of gravlax to each plate, layer with ¼ of the grated cucumber, and drizzle again with vinaigrette. Cover with the remaining gravlax and top with the sliced shiitakes. Drizzle with the remaining vinaigrette.

GRAVLAX
Calories 174;   Protein 24 g/94 cal;   Carbohydrates 10 g/41 cal;
Fat 4 g/39 cal;   (Saturated Fat 1 g/9 cal);   Cholesterol 84 mg;
Sodium 1257 mg;   Fiber 1 g;   Iron 13% of Daily Value

NAPOLEON
Calories 174;   Protein 23 g/90 cal;   Carbohydrates 6 g/22 cal;
Fat 7 g/62 cal;   (Saturated Fat 1 g/12 cal);   Cholesterol 26 mg;
Sodium 345 mg;   Fiber 2 g;   Vitamin A 29% of Daily Value

CILANTRO VINAIGRETTE
Calories 56;   Protein 1 g/3 cal;   Carbohydrates 2 g/8 cal;
Fat 5 g/46 cal;   (Saturated Fat 0 g/0 cal);   Cholesterol 0 mg;
Sodium 130 mg;   Fiber 0 g;   Vitamin C 26% of Daily Value

BABY LETTUCE SALAD WITH WHITE AND RED RADISHES AND HERB DRESSING*

2 teaspoons lemon juice
Sea salt and freshly ground black pepper
3 tablespoons extra-virgin olive oil
2 tablespoons mixed, chopped fresh herbs
　such as basil, thyme, mint, oregano,
　chives, or dill

½ – ¾ pounds assorted baby lettuces or mesclun
　mix, washed and spun dry
8 white radishes, trimmed
8 red radishes, trimmed

This is a clear vinaigrette, so you should mix it by hand.

Radishes are the first spring crop we receive from our farmers. Radishes have a spicy, earthy flavor I love. When I was growing up, my mother often sliced them paper thin and layered them on buttered dark brown sourdough bread as a snack for me and my sisters.

Use a fork to mix the lemon juice with the salt and pepper in a small bowl. Add the olive oil and fresh herbs.

ASSEMBLY: Put the baby lettuces into a bowl and toss with vinaigrette. Divide the lettuces among 4 luncheon plates. Put 2 red radishes and 2 white on each plate.

BABY LETTUCE SALAD
Calories 106;　Protein 2 g/7 cal;　Carbohydrates 3 g/13 cal;
Fat 10 g/86 cal;　(Saturated Fat 0 g/0 cal);　Cholesterol 0 mg;
Sodium 12 mg;　Fiber 2 g;　Vitamin C 59% of Daily Value

Chicken Breast with Couscous-Eggplant-Goat Cheese Stuffing, Moroccan Tomato Sauce, Spaghetti Squash, Red Chard, and Green Beans

MOROCCAN TOMATO SAUCE ✳

Have you ever tasted harissa? It is a hot sauce from North Africa and is wonderful on couscous, goulash, Serbian bean soup, and steak tartare. I love spicy foods.

Raz el hanout or ras il hanouf is the Moroccan equivalent of Asian five-spice powder or Indian garam masala. It combines the most characteristic spices of the Moroccan cuisine and is a mixture of about ten sweet and savory spices including cardamom, mace, nutmeg, cinnamon, allspice, and clove.

2 tablespoons olive oil
3 tablespoons chopped shallots
3 tablespoons chopped garlic
2 pounds tomatoes, coarsely chopped or a
    28-ounce can Italian plum tomatoes
1 teaspoon harissa sauce, available at specialty
    stores, or ½ teaspoon dried red pepper
    flakes mixed with ½ teaspoon cumin

½ teaspoon raz el hanout or garam masala, both
    available at specialty stores or see recipe on
    page 174 or ½ teaspoon powdered cumin
Sea salt

Heat the olive oil in a medium saucepan. Add the shallots and garlic and sauté for 2 – 3 minutes. Add the tomatoes, harissa, raz el hanout, and season to taste with salt.

Simmer for 15 minutes or until thickened. Cool for 5 minutes. Purée in a blender until smooth.

SPAGHETTI SQUASH

Sometimes we get orangetti squash, an orange spaghetti squash with a rich yellow color that dramatically contrasts with the dark chard and light green beans.

1 spaghetti squash (3 pounds)
1 cup water
2 teaspoons olive oil

1 tablespoon chopped chives or mint
Sea salt and freshly ground black pepper

Preheat the oven to 400° F.

Cut the squash in half lengthwise and scrape out the seeds. Place the squash, cut-side-down, in a baking dish. Add the water and bake about 45 minutes, or until you can easily insert the tip of a knife.

Remove the squash from the oven and, using a fork, scrape out the stringy pulp. It will separate into spaghetti-like strands. Put the squash into a serving bowl, season with olive oil, chives or mint, and salt and pepper to taste.

GREEN BEANS AND RED CHARD

Chard is a relative of the beet and should be treated as two vegetables. The stalk can be stir-fried or sautéed with olive

½ pound green beans, washed and strings
    removed
1 pound red or green chard, washed and
    stemmed

2 teaspoons olive oil
Sea salt and freshly ground black pepper

Steam the green beans for 4 – 5 minutes or until tender. Season to taste with 1 teaspoon olive oil and salt and pepper.

Steam the chard for 2 minutes or until bright green and softened. Season with the remaining olive oil and salt and pepper to taste.

oil, garlic, and other seasonings such as orange. Cut the leaves in julienne and sauté them in olive oil or else steam them and toss with olive oil and season with salt and pepper.

Chard is high in calcium, iron, and Vitamin A. I always feel that I am eating something earthy when I have chard or other cooked greens.

The stuffing keeps the chicken breasts moist while cooking, and they look beautiful when sliced. Stuffed chicken breast is so popular at Nora's that over the years we have developed over 50 different stuffing mixtures.

Tossing the couscous with the oil before cooking is a great trick. It keeps the couscous from sticking together.

Couscous is a precooked Moroccan pasta made of semolina. It is available in specialty stores and these days in large supermarkets, too.

A farmer in Pennsylvania raises chickens for us. They run free in big barns, have access to the outside, drink water from a well, and eat only organic feed.

¹/₂ cup couscous
2 tablespoons olive oil
Sea salt
1 cup water
2 tablespoons minced shallots
1 tablespoon minced garlic
¹/₂ pound eggplant, cut into ¹/₄-inch cubes
1 small red pepper, seeded, cored, and diced

¹/₂ teaspoon ground cumin
2 tablespoons chopped cilantro
2 ounces goat cheese, cut into ¹/₄-inch cubes
Freshly ground black pepper

Four 8-ounce boneless chicken breasts, wings attached (optional), with as much skin as possible left on.

Put the couscous in a small bowl, add 1 teaspoon olive oil, and toss to coat well. Bring 1 cup salted water to a boil. Add the couscous, return to a boil, and remove from the heat. Cover and steep for 5 minutes. Uncover and fluff with a fork to separate the grains.

Heat 1 tablespoon of the olive oil in a medium sauté pan, add the shallot and garlic, and sauté for 1 minute. Add the eggplant and cook for 5 minutes or until soft, stirring often. Add the red pepper and cumin and sauté 1 more minute. Remove from the heat, mix with the couscous, cilantro, and goat cheese. Taste and adjust the seasonings.

Preheat the oven to 375° F.

Divide the stuffing into 4 portions. Cut a pocket into the thick side of each chicken breast and stuff with half of each portion of stuffing. Put the remaining stuffing under the skin, pulling and tucking the skin to enclose the breast meat and stuffing. Brush the breast with the remaining oil and season with salt and pepper.

Roast the chicken breasts for 25 – 35 minutes or until cooked through and nicely browned. Remove from the oven, cover with aluminum foil to keep warm, and let rest for 2 – 3 minutes before serving and slicing.

ASSEMBLY: Pool some of the Moroccan tomato sauce on 4 dinner plates. Slice each chicken breast into 4 or 5 pieces and use a spatula to transfer them to the plates. Mound the spaghetti squash, red chard, and green beans around the chicken.

TOMATO SAUCE
Calories 141;   Protein 3 g/11 cal;   Carbohydrates 16 g/62 cal;   Fat 8 g/68 cal;   (Saturated Fat 1 g/10 cal);   Cholesterol 0 mg;   Sodium 23 mg;   Fiber 3 g;   Vitamin C 80% of Daily Value

SPAGHETTI SQUASH
Calories 161;   Protein 3 g/13 cal;   Carbohydrates 30 g/120 cal;   Fat 3 g/28 cal;   (Saturated Fat 1 g/7 cal);   Cholesterol 0 mg;   Sodium 6 mg;   Fiber 10 g;   Vitamin C 62% of Daily Value

GREEN BEANS AND CHARD
Calories 74;   Protein 3 g/12 cal;   Carbohydrates 8 g/33cal;   Fat 3 g/29 cal;   (Saturated Fat .7 g/6 cal);   Cholesterol 0 mg;   Sodium 264 mg;   Fiber 3 g;   Iron 21% of Daily Value

CHICKEN BREAST WITH STUFFING
Calories 507;   Protein 62 g/249 cal;   Carbohydrates 25 g/100 cal;   Fat 18 g/158 cal;   (Saturated Fat 4 g/48 cal);   Cholesterol 167 mg;   Sodium 186 mg;   Fiber 6 g;   Iron 19% of Daily Value

STRAWBERRY RHUBARB PIE WITH GINGER ICE CREAM

GINGER ICE CREAM ✳

You will need an ice cream maker.

½ cup sugar
½ cup water

3-inch piece of ginger
3 egg yolks
3 cups heavy cream
Fresh mint or lemon balm for garnish

At Nora's we use a vegetable juicer to squeeze the ginger. Ginger ice cream has a nice balance between spicy and sweet.

Pour the sugar into a small saucepan, add the water, and stir to dissolve. Boil the sugar and water for about 10 minutes or until it registers 220° F on a thermometer. Set aside. Do not touch or stir the sugar while it is boiling or crystals may form and ruin the syrup.

Grate or shred the ginger by hand or in a mini chopper. Put it in a double layer of cheesecloth and squeeze to make 1 tablespoon or more of juice.

Whip the egg yolks in an electric mixer or by hand with a balloon whip until lemon yellow and fluffy, about 5 minutes. While the mixer is running, carefully pour the hot sugar syrup along the side of the bowl, avoiding the beaters which will splatter the syrup.

Whip for about 1 minute. Reduce the mixer speed to low and add the cream and the ginger juice and beat until combined. Refrigerate the ice cream base until cool.

Pour this ginger custard into an ice cream machine and follow manufacturer's directions for freezing. Serves 8.

2 cups organic, unbleached white flour

1 tablespoon sugar

Pinch salt

2 sticks unsalted butter, cut into ¼-inch cubes

1½ – 2 tablespoons ice water

1 egg yolk mixed with 2 teaspoons milk for egg wash

This pie crust can be used for any kind of fruit pie. Omitting the sugar and adding a pinch of salt transforms it into a savory crust for a goat cheese tart, or wild mushroom and leek tart, (page 198). You can also roll out the dough and cut it with a cookie cutter into 3-inch rounds for making shortcakes with fresh berries and whipped cream.

Ramon Viera is the pastry chef at Nora's. He makes a wonderful flaky crust and his method of rolling the overhanging dough to form the edge of the pie gives it a beautiful look and stable edge. His pies have structure and the filling oozes out from the cut sides forming pools of warm fruit on our white plates.

Mix the flour, sugar, and salt in a medium bowl. Work the butter into the flour until it forms pea-sized pieces. You can also make the dough in a food processor using an on and off motion. Be careful not to overwork the dough or it will become too uniform—like a fine cornmeal—and your crust will not be flaky.

Add enough water to make the dough stick together. Press into a ball and wrap in plastic wrap. Refrigerate, to relax the dough, for at least 30 minutes.

Roll out the dough on a cool, flat surface to about ¼-inch thickness. Put a 9-inch pie pan upside down on the surface of the dough and cut a circle 3-inches larger than the pan. Turn the pie pan over and put the dough in it, pressing and shaping to fit. There will be extra dough hanging over the edge. Gather the remaining dough together and roll out again.

Cut the remaining dough into twelve to fourteen ¼-inch wide strips. Lay the strips on a cookie sheet and put them and the pie-pan dough in the freezer for 5 to 7 minutes or in the refrigerator for ½ hour to firm them before continuing.

STRAWBERRY-RHUBARB FILLING *

6 cups rhubarb (6 medium stalks), cut into ½-inch slices

1¼ cups sugar

2 pints strawberries, washed and hulled

2 tablespoons arrowroot or cornstarch

1 tablespoon grated orange rind

Preheat the oven to 375° F.

Put the rhubarb into a bowl, add the sugar, and toss to combine. Steep the rhubarb for 40 minutes or longer until it releases its juices. Drain in a colander and set aside. Cut the strawberries in halves or quarters, depending upon their size, and add them to the rhubarb. Sprinkle the fruit mixture with the arrowroot and grated orange peel and toss to combine.

Remove the pie shell and strips from the freezer or refrigerator. Fill the pie shell with the rhubarb-strawberry mixture.

Place 5 or 6 strips of dough over the filling. Interweave the remaining strips under and over these strips to form a lattice. Trim the ends. Roll the overhanging dough up and over the rim of the pie pan to form a thick rolled border. Crimp to form an attractive edge.

Brush the pie with the egg wash. Bake for 45 minutes or until the fruit is liquid and bubbling and the crust is golden. Allow the pie to cool for 10 minutes before slicing.

ASSEMBLY: Put a slice of pie on each of 4 dessert plates with a big scoop of ginger ice cream. Garnish with a sprig of mint or lemon balm. Serves 8.

GINGER ICE CREAM (1 OUNCE)
Calories 86;   Protein 1 g/4 cal;   Carbohydrates 3 g/12 cal;
Fat 8 g/72 cal;   (Saturated Fat 2 g/20 cal);   Cholesterol 46 mg;
Sodium 8 mg;   Fiber 0 g;   Vitamin A 14% of Daily Value

STRWABERRY-RHUBARB FILLING
Calories 168;   Protein 2 g/8 cal;   Carbohydrates 43 g/172 cal;
Fat 0 g/0 cal;   (Saturated Fat 0 g/0 cal);   Cholesterol 0 mg;
Sodium 140 mg;   Fiber 4 g;   Vitamin C 89% of Daily Value

PIE CRUST
Calories 333;   Protein 4 g/15 cal;   Carbohydrates 26 g/102 cal;
Fat 24 g/216 cal;   (Saturated Fat 15 g/132 cal);   Cholesterol 89 mg;
Sodium 31 mg;   Fiber 1 g;   Vitamin A 25% of Daily Value

SPRING MENU IV

Sautéed Virginia Morels and Spinach with Goat Cheese and Beet Vinaigrette

Grilled Maine Salmon in Lemongrass Broth with Pad Thai Noodles, Shiitakes, Carrots, Spring Onions,
and Tat Soi

Stonebridge Farm Baby Lettuce with Edible Flowers and Raspberry Vinaigrette

Strawberry Shortcake with Light Whipped Cream

WINE SELECTIONS

*A crisp dry German or Alsatian Riesling would be a perfect companion to this menu. The delicate flavors
of morels, salmon, and shiitakes need a crisp, full-flavored wine.*

Alsatian: Marcel Deiss Riesling 1989

German: Weingut Wittman Spätlese Halbtrocken 1990

SAUTÉED VIRGINIA MORELS AND SPINACH WITH GOAT CHEESE AND BEET VINAIGRETTE

BEET VINAIGRETTE *

4 large shallots, peeled
1 teaspoon olive oil
Sea salt and freshly ground black pepper
4 small beets, about 4 ounces each, greens trimmed

⅛ teaspoon caraway seeds
1 tablespoon red wine vinegar
¾ cup water
¼ cup canola oil

Preheat the oven to 400° F.

Put the shallots in a small, non-reactive baking dish. Dress with 1 teaspoon olive oil and season with salt and pepper. Cover with aluminum foil and roast for 30 – 40 minutes or until soft.

Steam or boil the beets for 15 – 20 minutes in a small saucepan. Peel the beets while still warm and put them in a blender with the roasted shallots, caraway seeds, vinegar, and just enough water to cover the blades, about ½ cup. Add salt and pepper to taste.

Purée the ingredients and, with the machine running, add the oil in a thin stream, blending until emulsified. Add the remaining water, if necessary, to thin the vinaigrette to the consistency of heavy cream.

SAUTÉED VIRGINIA MORELS WITH SPINACH AND GOAT CHEESE

1 tablespoon olive oil
2 tablespoons minced shallots
2 tablespoons minced garlic
½ pound morels, washed and dried
Sea salt and freshly ground black pepper

1½ – 2 tablespoons sherry, white wine, or balsamic vinegar
6 ounces spinach, stemmed, washed, and drained
4 ounces goat cheese, cut in ¼-inch cubes

Wash the mushrooms by immersing them in a large basin of cold water and draining them on kitchen or paper towels. Do this quickly; otherwise they become soggy.

Heat the olive oil in a medium sauté pan. Add shallots and garlic and sauté for 2 – 3 minutes. Lower the heat, add the morels, and continue sautéing for about 3 minutes, stirring from time to time until the morels are softened. Season to taste with salt and pepper.

Beet vinaigrette is a beautiful, tasty sauce, and I use it with sautéed or grilled sea scallops, grilled portobello mushrooms, crabmeat salad, or even a smoked trout and apple pasta.

I enjoy all kinds of wild mushrooms. As a child in Austria, I used to go mushroom-hunting every fall with my parents and sisters. I loved doing it, even though my older sisters were more successful than I.

In May, morels are plentiful close to Washington, DC. Recently, I joined some friends on a mushroom hunt in the Virginia countryside. We stopped for pizza on the way home and asked the cook to use the fresh morels on our pizzas.

I serve morels or chanterelles, sautéed with watercress or dandelion greens, on toasted garlic bread, as a bruschetta, (page 117), and drizzle it with a balsamic vinaigrette. Delicious!

Add the sherry, wine, or balsamic vinegar, raise the heat, and cook for 2 more minutes or until most of the liquid has evaporated. Stir in the spinach and sauté briefly, just until wilted. Remove from the heat.

ASSEMBLY: Divide the beet vinaigrette among 4 luncheon plates. Arrange the morel and spinach mixture on top. Garnish each salad with goat cheese. Serve warm.

BEET VINAIGRETTE
Calories 110;   Protein 1 g/5 cal;   Carbohydrates 10 g/41 cal;
Fat 7 g/64 cal;   (Saturated Fat .5 g/5 cal);   Cholesterol 0 mg;
Sodium 45 mg;   Fiber 2 g;   Vitamin C 16% of Daily Value

SAUTEED VIRGINIA MORELS WITH SPINACH
AND GOAT CHEESE
Calories 242;   Protein 9 g/36 cal;   Carbohydrates 36 g/145 cal;
Fat 7 g/61 cal;   (Saturated Fat 3 g/29 cal);   Cholesterol 17 mg;
Sodium 76 mg;   Fiber 7 g;   Vitamin A 64% of Daily Value

Grilled Maine Salmon in Lemongrass Broth with Pad Thai Noodles, Shiitakes, Carrots, Spring Onions, and Tat Soi

G R I L L E D   M A I N E   S A L M O N   I N   L E M O N G R A S S   B R O T H *

4 ounces Pad Thai noodles or rice sticks

3-inch piece of ginger, peeled and sliced

3 stalks lemongrass, outer leaves removed and thinly sliced

4 Kaffir lime leaves or 2 tablespoons fresh lime juice (optional)

1 – 2 jalapeño chilies or to taste

6 cups water

2 tablespoons nuoc mam or Thai fish sauce

2 large carrots, about 6 ounces, peeled and thinly sliced

16 shiitakes, about 3 ounces, washed, stemmed, and quartered

4 green onions, trimmed and sliced thinly on the diagonal

4 ounces tat soi or watercress, stems trimmed

1/2 cup cilantro leaves for garnish

4 salmon fillets, skinned, about 6 ounces each

1 teaspoon canola oil

Here I take the Asian concept of a fish soup and elevate it by presenting the broth as a base for a whole fillet of salmon. This dish also works with scallops, shrimp, or crabmeat. I always try to get my fish from cold waters because they are often less polluted and produce healthier fish. Most of my salmon are from Alaska, Iceland, or Maine.

Preheat the grill or broiler.

Soak the rice sticks in hot tap water for 3 minutes or until softened. Drain.

Mince the ginger, lemongrass, lime leaves, and chilies finely by hand or in a small chopper. Bring the water to a boil in a medium saucepan and add the ginger, lemongrass, lime leaves, and chilies. Season to taste with nuoc mam. Add the carrots, shiitakes, green onions, and the drained noodles. Simmer about 1 minute. The broth can be made ahead to this point. Just before serving, stir in the tat soi or watercress. This will keep them green and crisp.

Brush the salmon with the oil and grill or broil 3 minutes per side or until the fish turns opaque and medium rare.

ASSEMBLY: Ladle the broth into 4 large soup bowls, dividing the vegetables and noodles evenly. Top with the salmon and garnish with cilantro.

In this dish, you want to make every vegetable look as pretty as possible.

The Asian ingredients in this recipe are available at Asian markets and specialty stores.

The amount of fish sauce you use depends upon how much your palate likes salt.

GRILLED MAINE SALMON IN LEMONGRASS BROTH WITH PAD THAI NOODLES, SHIITAKES, CARROTS, SPRING ONIONS, AND TAT SOI

Calories 345;   Protein 40 g/161 cal;   Carbohydrates 23 g/91 cal; Fat 10 g/93 cal;   (Saturated Fat 2 g/21 cal);   Cholesterol 66 mg; Sodium 675 mg;   Fiber 2 g;   Iron 23% of Daily Value

STONEBRIDGE FARM BABY LETTUCE SALAD WITH EDIBLE FLOWERS AND RASPBERRY VINAIGRETTE

RASPBERRY VINAIGRETTE ✳

You can make a vinaigrette with any other fruit. Try it with mangoes, oranges, papaya, or strawberries. And you don't have to serve these vinaigrettes just with lettuce. Try grilled chicken breast with a mango-lime vinaigrette or grilled swordfish with papaya-lime vinaigrette.

The best way to store washed greens is in the refrigerator in a plastic bag interspersed with paper towels. This keeps them crisp and prevents them from spoiling.

I think nasturtiums are one of the best tasting flowers. They are peppery like watercress or radishes.

If you cannot find fresh raspberries, substitute a good quality raspberry vinegar and correct the seasoning.

3 ounces fresh raspberries
1 teaspoon lemon juice
¼ cup orange juice

2 tablespoons canola oil
Sea salt and freshly ground black pepper

½ pound baby lettuce or mesclun mix, washed and spun dry
16 nasturtiums, if available
8 pansies or 16 violets, if available

Purée the raspberries, citrus juices, and canola oil in the blender until smooth and emulsified. Add salt and pepper to taste.

Wash the flowers by floating them in a large basin of water. Spin or pat dry with care. They are delicate. Refrigerate to keep fresh until ready to use.

ASSEMBLY: Toss the lettuces with raspberry vinaigrette. Put them on 4 luncheon plates. Divide the flowers evenly among the plates and serve.

RASPBERRY VINAIGRETTE
Calories 81;   Protein .25 g/1 cal;   Carbohydrates 4 g/17 cal;
Fat 7 g/63 cal;   (Saturated Fat .4 g/4 cal);   Cholesterol 0 mg;
Sodium 28 mg;   Fiber 1 g;   Vitamin C 22% of Daily Value

BABY LETTUCE SALAD WITH EDIBLE FLOWERS
Calories 46;   Protein 3 g/12 cal;   Carbohydrates 8 g/30 cal;
Fat .4 g/4 cal;   (Saturated Fat .1 g/1 cal);   Cholesterol 0 mg;
Sodium 68 mg;   Fiber 4 g;   Vitamin C 57% of Daily Value

STRAWBERRY SHORTCAKE WITH LIGHT WHIPPED CREAM

SHORTCAKE

This is a very soft biscuit dough. I use the same recipe for making a savory biscuit, but I omit the sugar and add some cracked black pepper and chopped fresh herbs, such as sage or thyme. These biscuits are delicious served with a stew or a ragout.

1⅓ cups all-purpose flour
2 to 3 tablespoons sugar
1 tablespoon baking powder
¼ teaspoon salt
6 tablespoons cold unsalted butter, cut into
    ¼-inch dice

½ cup milk
1 teaspoon lemon juice
½ teaspoon vanilla extract

Preheat oven to 375° F.

Line a medium sheet pan with aluminum foil or parchment paper.

Put the flour, 2 tablespoons of the sugar, baking powder, and salt in a medium bowl. Mix well or sift together. Add the butter and work it between your fingers until the texture resembles coarse crumbs. You can also prepare the dough in a food processor with an on and off pulsing motion until it has the same consistency.

Add the milk, lemon juice, and vanilla and stir with a fork to blend. The dough will be very soft.

Scoop 4 portions of the dough onto the prepared baking sheet using an ice cream scoop or a large spoon. Space the scoops 1 – 2 inches apart. Flatten each scoop into a 3½-inch circle and sprinkle with the remaining sugar. Bake 30 minutes or until golden and firm on the outside and cooked through.

CRUSHED STRAWBERRIES

This strawberry sauce is delicious with frozen yogurt or ice cream.

Nothing tastes more like spring than fresh, fragrant, local strawberries. I find, however, that many of my customers don't order strawberries because they have had so many that are tasteless. If it is spring, and the strawberries are local, be sure to order them. You won't be disappointed. This is what eating in season is all about.

2 pints strawberries, washed and hulled
2 tablespoons sugar

1 TABLESPOON GRAND MARNIER OR ORANGE JUICE
Fresh mint for garnish

Cut the strawberries into halves or quarters, depending on the size. Toss with the sugar and Grand Marnier or orange juice and set aside until the berries release some of their juices. Crush some of the berries with the back of a spoon to make the juices thicker. Garnish with mint.

LIGHT WHIPPED CREAM

2 egg whites
2 tablespoons powdered sugar

½ cup heavy cream

Put the egg whites into a medium bowl, add the sugar, and whip by hand or machine until the whites form firm but not dry peaks.

Whip the cream by hand or machine until it forms soft peaks. Fold the cream into the beaten egg whites.

ASSEMBLY: Split the shortcakes horizontally. Place the bottom half of each shortcake on a luncheon plate. Add some of the light whipped cream to each shortcake, then the strawberries and top with the remaining cream. Cover with the top half of the shortcake, placing it at a slight angle. Garnish with mint.

SHORTCAKE
Calories 278; Protein 5 g/18 cal; Carbohydrates 32 g/129 cal; Fat 15 g/131 cal; (Saturated Fat 9 g/81 cal); Cholesterol 39 mg; Sodium 370 mg; Fiber 1 g; Calcium 18% of Daily Value

CRUSHED STRAWBERRIES
Calories 81; Protein 1 g/4 cal; Carbohydrates 18 g/72 cal; Fat .6 g/5 cal; (Saturated Fat 0 g/0 cal); Cholesterol 0 mg; Sodium 2 mg; Fiber 3 g; Vitamin C 147% of Daily Value

LIGHT WHIPPED CREAM
Calories 123; Protein 2 g/9 cal; Carbohydrates 4 g/17 cal; Fat 11 g/97 cal; (Saturated Fat 7 g/62 cal); Cholesterol 41 mg; Sodium 39 mg; Fiber 0 g; Vitamin A 13% of Daily Value

SPRING MENU V

Asparagus and Virginia Morel Mushroom Salad with Roasted Garlic and Lemon Dressing

Grilled Lamb Chops with Rosemary Sauce, Wild Rice and Fennel Pilaf, and Baby Carrots

Spinach and Frisée Salad with Baby Beets and Hazelnut Vinaigrette

Peach-Strawberry Compote with Grand Marnier and Vanilla Ice Cream

WINE SELECTIONS

Pinot Noir works wonders here. Lamb, rosemary, and Pinot Noir offer a traditional blend of flavors.

Etude 1990 California

Domaine Serene 1990 Oregon

Asparagus and Virginia Morel Mushroom Salad with Roasted Garlic and Lemon Dressing

ROASTED GARLIC AND LEMON DRESSING ✳

1 head of garlic, unpeeled
Zested peel of 1 lemon
Juice from 1 lemon (2 ounces)
1 teaspoon Dijon mustard

1 green onion, coarsely chopped
½ cup olive oil
Sea salt and freshly ground pepper

Preheat the oven to 400° F.

Cut off the top ⅓ of the head of garlic exposing the inside of the cloves. Wrap the garlic in aluminum foil and bake for 30 – 40 minutes or until very soft.

Squeeze the garlic pulp into a blender. Zest the lemon and reserve for garnish. Pour the lemon juice into a measuring cup and add enough water to make ½ cup liquid. Pour the lemon-water mixture into the blender, and add mustard, the green onion, and salt and pepper to taste. Purée until smooth. While the machine is running, add the olive oil in a thin stream blending until the vinaigrette is emulsified.

ASPARAGUS

¾ pound asparagus, trimmed and peeled, if large

Steam or boil the asparagus for 4 minutes or until tender. The exact cooking time will depend upon the size of the asparagus. Drain in a colander and rinse with cold water to stop the cooking. Drain on a kitchen towel. Cut the bottom third of the asparagus stalks into ½-inch diagonal slices and set aside. Reserve the upper two-thirds.

VIRGINIA MOREL MUSHROOM SALAD

1 tablespoon olive oil
10 ounces morels, drained and trimmed
8 green onions, trimmed, sliced into ¼-inch
  rounds

2 teaspoons balsamic vinegar
1½ teaspoons tamari
Freshly ground black pepper
⅓ cup chopped flat leaf parsley for garnish

Heat the olive oil in a sauté pan, add the morels and sauté for 2 – 3 minutes. Add the green onions, balsamic vinegar, and tamari and continue sautéing for 2 more minutes, stirring from time to time, until soft and blended. Remove from the heat and add the sliced and cooked asparagus stems. Stir to combine. Season

Whenever I make this dressing, I make extra to use, with the addition of some fresh herbs, as a sauce for pasta or poached fish. You can substitute roasted, peeled garlic cloves for the head of garlic. I always have some roasted shallots and garlic on hand. I use them to thicken sauces or emulsify vinaigrettes made in a blender.

At Nora's, we keep at least 2 pots of water boiling to blanch vegetables. This way we can blanch individual servings, drain, and season quickly. We also have a large commercial steamer to help us stay abreast of the orders. For the home cook, a collapsible steamer insert or blanching in a saucepan works well.

Asparagus is great for quick stir-frying, sliced on the diagonal.

I love the woodsy taste of the morels and find many uses for them in my spring menus. I also serve this salad of asparagus and morels with a grilled chicken breast, veal or pork chop, or swordfish. When I taste spring lamb, morels, and asparagus, I know it is really spring!

to taste with pepper.

ASSEMBLY: Pour the garlic-lemon dressing in a pool covering one-half of each salad plate. Fan the asparagus spears over the dressing. Put a large spoonful of the morel and asparagus mixture at the base of each asparagus fan, dividing the portions evenly among the 4 plates. Sprinkle with parsley.

ROASTED GARLIC AND LEMON DRESSING
(1 Tablespoon)
Calories 83;   Protein .5 g/2 cal;   Carbohydrates 2 g/8 cal;
Fat 8 g/74 cal;   (Saturated Fat 1 g/12 cal);   Cholesterol 0 mg;
Sodium 37 mg;   Fiber 0 g;   Vitamin C 11% of Daily Value

VIRGINIA MOREL MUSHROOM SALAD
Calories 61;   Protein 2 g/7 cal;   Carbohydrates 5 g/21 cal;
Fat 4 g/33 cal;   (Saturated Fat .6 g/5 cal);   Cholesterol 0 mg;
Sodium 48 mg;   Fiber 1 g;   Vitamin C 24% of Daily Value

ASPARAGUS
Calories 20;   Protein 2 g/9 cal;   Carbohydrates 2 g/6 cal;
Fat .6 g/5 cal;   (Saturated Fat 0 g/0 cal);   Cholesterol 0 mg;
Sodium 11 mg;   Fiber 1 g;   Vitamin C 35% of Daily Value

GRILLED LAMB CHOPS WITH ROSEMARY SAUCE, WILD RICE AND FENNEL PILAF, AND BABY CARROTS

ROSEMARY SAUCE ✱

6 shallots, peeled
1 head garlic, separated into cloves and peeled
2 tablespoons tamari
2 teaspoons Dijon mustard
1 tablespoon rosemary needles

1 teaspoon sherry vinegar
½ cup white wine
⅓ cup plus 1 teaspoon olive oil
Sea salt and freshly ground pepper

This sauce also makes a good marinade, especially for leg of lamb. Try substituting another herb for the rosemary, such as basil, cilantro, or flat leaf parsley.

Preheat the oven to 400° F.

Put the shallots and garlic in a small roasting pan, add 1 teaspoon of the olive oil, and season to taste with salt and pepper. Cover with aluminum foil and roast the shallots and garlic for 30 – 40 minutes or until very soft.

Put the shallots and garlic into a blender. Add the tamari, mustard, rosemary, vinegar, and white wine. Process until smooth. While the machine is running, add the remaining olive oil in a thin stream and purée until emulsified. Season to taste with salt and pepper.

WILD RICE AND FENNEL PILAF

4 tablespoons minced shallots
1½ tablespoons olive oil
1½ teaspoon minced garlic
1 cup wild rice
1 cup white wine

3 cups water
1 fennel bulb, about ¾ pounds, fronds reserved for garnish
2 teaspoons balsamic vinegar
Sea salt and freshly ground pepper

Fennel has a refreshing anise flavor and tastes good eaten raw. Cut it into thin slices or sticks and serve as an appetizer.

You can make this wild rice a main course by adding a sauté of carrots, peppers, and greens plus pine nuts. Or give it a Chinese twist by using the cooked wild rice as a base for stir-fried rice with ginger and shiitake mushrooms.

Sauté the shallots in 1 tablespoon of the olive oil until softened. Add the garlic and rice and stir until coated with oil. Add the wine and 2½ cups of the water, season to taste with salt and pepper, and bring to a boil. Cover, reduce the heat, and simmer for about 35 minutes.

Remove from the heat and set aside until all the remaining liquid is absorbed, about 15 minutes.

Peel the tough strings from the outer ribs of the fennel. Cut the bulb in half and slice thinly across the stalks. Heat the remaining oil in a sauté pan.

Add the fennel and sauté, stirring frequently, for 1 minute. Add the remaining water and balsamic vinegar and simmer for 8 minutes, or until the fennel is soft and the liquid has evaporated.

Taste for seasoning. Add the fennel to the wild rice and stir to combine.

The first carrots of spring are so sweet, and they make a nutritious snack high in vitamin A.

16 baby carrots, about ¹/₂ pound, with green tops, greens trimmed to 1¹/₂-inches

Sea salt and freshly ground black pepper
1 teaspoon olive oil

Steam the carrots for 5 — 8 minutes or until crisp-tender. Season with salt and pepper and olive oil.

GRILLED LAMB CHOPS

I love the taste of our lamb. It is raised for us in Virginia and has no strong mutton flavor. Because we buy directly from a small farmer, we buy the entire animal, raised especially for us. At Nora's we use 3 — 4 whole lambs per week. This gives us many lamb chops and legs, but also a lot of ground lamb.

12 6-ounce rib lamb chops, 1 to 1¹/₂-inches thick, trimmed

1 tablespoon olive oil
Sea salt and freshly ground black pepper

Preheat the grill or broiler.

Brush the lamb chops with olive oil and season to taste with salt and pepper. Broil or grill them for 2 — 4 minutes per side for medium rare, or to taste.

ASSEMBLY: Pool the rosemary sauce in the center of 4 large dinner plates. Pile some wild rice pilaf in the center of each plate, lean three overlapping rib chops against the pilaf and arrange 4 baby carrots on the opposite side of the plates. Garnish with fennel fronds.

ROSEMARY SAUCE
Calories 226;   Protein 3 g/12 cal;   Carbohydrates 12 g/49 cal;
Fat 18 g/165 cal;   (Saturated Fat 3 g/23 cal);   Cholesterol 0 mg;
Sodium 482 mg;   Fiber 0 g;   Vitamin A 66% of Daily Value

BABY CARROTS
Calories 24;   Protein .5 g/2 cal;   Carbohydrates 5 g/21 cal;
Fat .1 g/1 cal;   (Saturated Fat 0 g/0 cal);   Cholesterol 0 mg;
Sodium 20 mg;   Fiber 2 g;   Vitamin C 199% of Daily Value

WILD RICE AND FENNEL PILAF
Calories 221;   Protein 9 g/35 cal;   Carbohydrates 37 g/149 cal;
Fat 4 g/37 cal;   (Saturated Fat .6 g/5 cal);   Cholesterol 0 mg;
Sodium 74 mg;   Fiber 1 g;   Iron 23% of Daily Value

GRILLED LAMB CHOPS
Calories 356;   Protein 40 g/160 cal;   Carbohydrates .25 g/1 cal;
Fat 22 g/195 cal;   (Saturated Fat 7 g/64 cal);   Cholesterol 129 mg;
Sodium 174 mg;   Fiber 0 g;   Iron 21% of Daily Value

SPINACH AND FRISÉE SALAD WITH BABY BEETS AND HAZELNUT VINAIGRETTE

HAZELNUT VINAIGRETTE ✳

If you don't have hazelnut oil in the house, toast 4 tablespoons of hazelnuts in a 325° oven until dry, about 10 minutes. Let them cool. Remove the dark outer skin, and make the vinaigrette in the blender substituting canola oil for the hazelnut oil. Add the hazelnuts to the blender, turning the machine on and off to chop them coarsely.

¹/₂ tablespoon white wine vinegar
Sea salt and freshly ground black pepper

2 tablespoons hazelnut oil
1 tablespoon minced chives

Put the vinegar in a small bowl with salt and pepper to taste. Stir to dissolve. Whisk in the oil, add the chives, and taste for seasoning.

16 baby beets, greens trimmed to 1-inch
4 ounces spinach, stemmed, washed, and
    spun dry

½ pound frisée, trimmed, washed, and spun dry

I always cook more beets than necessary, since they are so handy as a base for a vinaigrette or as a relish with some apples.

Steam the beets for 12 – 15 minutes in a small, covered saucepan using a collapsible steamer. As soon as the beets are cool enough to handle, peel and toss the beets in a bowl with a tablespoon of the vinaigrette.

Tear the spinach and frisée into 2-inch pieces and put into a medium bowl.

ASSEMBLY: Pour the remaining vinaigrette over the greens and toss to coat evenly. Divide the greens among four luncheon plates and add 4 baby beets to each plate.

HAZELNUT VINAIGRETTE
Calories 42;   Protein 0 g/0 cal;   Carbohydrates .25 g/1 cal;
Fat 5 g/41 cal;   (Saturated Fat .1 g/1 cal);   Cholesterol 0 mg;
Sodium 54 mg;   Fiber 0 g;   Vitamin C 1% of Daily Value

BEETS
Calories 50;   Protein 2 g/7 cal;   Carbohydrates 11 g/42 cal;
Fat .1 g/1 cal;   (Saturated Fat 0 g/0 cal);   Cholesterol 0 mg;
Sodium 82 mg;   Fiber 4 g;   Iron 6% of Daily Value

SPINACH AND FRISÉE
Calories 18;   Protein 2 g/7 cal;   Carbohydrates 2 g/9 cal;
Fat .2 g/2 cal;   (Saturated Fat 0 g/0 cal);   Cholesterol 0 mg;
Sodium 27 mg;   Fiber 2 g;   Vitamin C 35% of Daily Value

PEACH-STRAWBERRY COMPOTE WITH GRAND MARNIER AND VANILLA ICE CREAM

PEACH-STRAWBERRY COMPOTE

This compote is versatile and can be served with ginger ice cream (page 43), chocolate sorbet (page 137), plain low-fat yogurt, frozen yogurt, or sorbets. It is also good with lemon poppy seed cake (page 194).

You can substitute other fruits in the compote such as plums, raspberries, or cherries with peaches.

I don't like to peel organic fruit, and since this compote cooks the peaches for only a short time, their skins won't come off and float unappealingly in the juice.

Juice of 1 orange
Juice of ½ lemon
2 tablespoons sugar
Peel of 1 orange, minced
1 tablespoon Grand Marnier

6 firm peaches (2 pounds), washed and sliced
1 pint strawberries (¾ pound), washed, hulled, and quartered
Fresh mint for garnish

Pour the juice of the orange and the ½ lemon into a measuring cup and add enough water to make ½ cup liquid, if necessary. Pour this mixture into a medium saucepan, add the sugar, and cook 5 minutes or until thickened and syrupy.

Add the orange peel, Grand Marnier, and sliced peaches. Return to a boil, then reduce the heat and simmer 2 – 3 minutes, until the peaches are tender.

Add the strawberries, remove from the heat, and stir, carefully, to combine.

You will need an ice cream maker.

¹/₂ cup sugar
¹/₂ cup water
3 egg yolks

3 cups heavy cream
3-inch piece of vanilla bean, cut in half length-
*   wise with seeds scraped out or 1 tablespoon*
*   vanilla extract*

Pour the sugar into a small saucepan, add the water, and stir to dissolve. Boil the sugar for about 10 minutes or until it reaches 220° F on a thermometer. Do not touch or stir the sugar while it is boiling or crystals may form and ruin the syrup.

Whip the egg yolks in a mixer until lemon yellow and fluffy, about 5 minutes. While the mixer is running, carefully pour the hot sugar syrup along the side of the bowl, avoiding the beaters which will splatter the syrup. Whip about 1 minute. Reduce the mixer speed to low, add the cream and vanilla, and beat until combined. Refrigerate the ice cream base until cool.

Pour the ice cream base into an ice cream maker and follow manufacturer's directions for freezing.

ASSEMBLY: Put 1 – 2 scoops of ice cream into each dessert bowl. Pour some of the warm compote over each serving and garnish with mint. Serves 8.

The warm compote and cold ice cream makes a perfect combination. This custard, minus the vanilla, is an ice cream base that can be used for all different flavors. For instance, add 2 tablespoons ginger juice for ginger ice cream, 4 ounces melted chocolate for chocolate ice cream, 2 tablespoons maple syrup for maple ice cream, 1 tablespoon lemon juice for lemon ice cream, or any kind of fruit purée.

PEACH-STRAWBERRY COMPOTE
Calories 199;   Protein 3 g/11 cal;   Carbohydrates 46 g/182 cal;
Fat .7 g/6 cal;   (Saturated Fat 0 g/0 cal);   Cholesterol 0 mg;
Sodium 3 mg;   Fiber 7 g;   Vitamin A 21% of Daily Value

VANILLA ICE CREAM (1 OUNCE)
Calories 89;   Protein 1 g/3 cal;   Carbohydrates 4 g/14 cal;
Fat 8 g/72 cal;   (Saturated Fat 5 g/44 cal);   Cholesterol 46 mg;
Sodium 8 mg;   Fiber 0 g;   Vitamin A 11% of Daily Value

SUMMER

SUMMER MENU I

Grilled Eggplant, Tomato, and Fresh Mozzarella Salad with Basil Vinaigrette

Mussel, Shrimp, and Sea Scallop Bouillabaisse with Aioli Croutons

Baby Head Lettuces with Watermelon, Honeydew, Cantaloupe, and Lime Dressing

Meringue with Mango Sorbet and Raspberries

WINE SELECTIONS
*Rosé and bouillabaisse were meant for one another! A crisp,
dry, full-bodied Rosé from the Provence region of France makes for the perfect marriage.*

Domaine Ott 1991 Provence

Domaine Richeaume 1991 Provence

GRILLED EGGPLANT, TOMATO, AND FRESH MOZZARELLA SALAD WITH BASIL VINAIGRETTE

2 tablespoons tamari

2 tablespoons olive oil

Freshly ground black pepper

1 pound eggplant, cut into twelve ½-inch thick rounds

1 pound tomatoes, cut into twelve ¼-inch thick rounds

½ pound mozzarella, cut into twelve ¼-inch rounds

¾ cup basil vinaigrette (substitute basil for cilantro in the recipe on page 37)

Basil sprigs for garnish

A mixture of tamari, olive oil, and pepper is an easy marinade for any vegetable you might choose to grill.

Sometimes I also add 2 tablespoons of balsamic vinaigrette to the marinade.

Preheat the grill or broiler.

Mix the tamari, olive oil, and pepper together in a bowl to make the marinade. Brush the eggplant with the marinade and grill or broil it for 1 – 2 minutes per side or until browned and soft.

ASSEMBLY: Make a pool of basil vinaigrette on each of 4 luncheon plates. Alternate slices of eggplant, tomato, and mozzarella in a circle on top of the dressing. Garnish each salad with basil sprigs.

Croutons or toasts make a nice appetizer spread with some paté, a tapenade, a purée of white beans, chopped tomato salad, or fresh goat cheese.

GRILLED EGGPLANT, TOMATO, AND FRESH
MOZZARELLA SALAD
Calories 276;   Protein 19 g/74 cal;   Carbohydrates 13 g/52 cal;
Fat 17 g/150 cal;   (Saturated Fat 1 g/9 cal);   Cholesterol 30 mg;
Sodium 509 mg;   Fiber 3 g;   Calcium 54% of Daily Value

MUSSEL, SHRIMP, AND SEA SCALLOP BOUILLABAISE WITH AIOLI CROUTONS

Twelve ½-inch thick slices from a loaf of French bread

Preheat the oven to 425° F.

Place the bread slices on a baking sheet and toast in the oven for 15 minutes or until crisp. Remove and cool. You can also toast the bread in a toaster.

Use aioli as a dipping sauce with vegetables or on grilled or broiled fish. It is also delicious with steamed potatoes. If you want to omit the egg yolk, substitute 1 tablespoon of Dijon mustard.

AIOLI　✳

Variations include: herb mayonnaise made by adding 1 – 2
tablespoons chopped fresh herbs;
green mayonnaise made by
adding 1 tablespoon spinach
purée (steamed spinach, squeezed
dry and puréed); tomato mayonnaise made by adding 1
tablespoon tomato purée; and
chili mayonnaise made by
adding 1 teaspoon of hot
chili paste.

3 to 4 cloves garlic
1/2 teaspoon salt
1 egg yolk

1/2 cup olive oil
2 teaspoons lemon juice
Freshly ground black pepper

Mix the garlic and salt on a cutting board by mashing them together very well using the side of a knife blade.

Place the small bowl in which you will whisk the aioli on a wet paper towel to prevent it from slipping. Put the egg yolk and the mashed garlic and salt into the bowl. Beat until lemony in color.

Add the olive oil, drop by drop, whisking continuously, until the sauce begins to thicken. Whisk in the remaining oil in a slow stream. Add the lemon juice and pepper to taste. If the aioli is too thick, add a few drops of water to thin it.

MUSSEL, SHRIMP, AND SEA SCALLOP BOUILLABAISSE

There are two tricks to making a bouillabaisse properly: the liquid must boil to emulsify the olive oil and thicken the soup, and the seafood should be added at the end to avoid over-cooking. Remember, the soup retains its warmth and keeps cooking the shellfish even after it leaves the heat.

At Nora's we often make this soup without the shellfish, pour it into a large, flat soup bowl and top it with a grilled fillet of fish garnished with a dollop of aioli.

4 tablespoons olive oil
2 carrots, peeled and minced
2 ribs celery, minced
2 leeks, white part only, washed and minced
1 teaspoon minced garlic
1 teaspoon fennel seeds
6 – 8 saffron threads
Grated peel of 1/2 orange
Pinch cayenne
2 teaspoons minced flat leaf parsley
1 teaspoon thyme
2 bay leaves

1/2 teaspoon sea salt and freshly ground black pepper
1 1/2 cups white wine
1 1/2 pounds tomatoes, peeled, seeded, and chopped or a 28-ounce can Italian tomatoes, drained and chopped

20 mussels, scrubbed clean and beards removed
3/4 pound shrimp, shelled and deveined
3/4 pound sea scallops
Rosemary, thyme, and basil sprigs for garnish

Rinse the sea scallops and remove the tough foot.

Heat 4 tablespoons of olive oil in a large saucepan. Add the carrots, celery, and leeks and sauté for about 4 minutes. Add the garlic, fennel seeds, saffron, orange peel, cayenne, parsley, thyme, bay leaves, and salt and pepper. Sauté for 1 – 2 minutes or until the herbs and spices are fragrant.

Add the wine and tomatoes and bring to a boil. Add the mussels, cover the pot, and return to a boil. Add the shrimp and scallops and stir to combine. Cover and cook for 2 minutes or until the mussels are open and the shrimp and scallops are opaque but barely cooked through.

ASSEMBLY: Spread the aioli on the toasts. Divide the soup among four large bowls, distributing the broth and shellfish equally. Garnish with the toasts and fresh herbs.

AIOLI CROUTONS

Calories 324;   Protein 3 g/11 cal;   Carbohydrates 14 g/56 cal;
Fat 29 g/257 cal;   (Saturated Fat 4 g/35 cal);   Cholesterol 53 mg;
Sodium 411 mg;   Fiber 1 g;   Iron 8% of Daily Value

BOUILLABAISSE

Calories 504;   Protein 53 g/210 cal;   Carbohydrates 32 g/126 cal;
Fat 19 g/168 cal;   (Saturated Fat 2 g/21 cal);   Cholesterol 258 mg;
Sodium 995 mg;   Fiber 5 g;   Calcium 32% of Daily Value

BABY HEAD LETTUCES WITH WATERMELON, HONEYDEW, CANTALOUPE, AND LIME DRESSING*

This salad was inspired by the way I like to serve melon—with a wedge of lime and a garnish of mint. It is not an earth-shattering new flavor combination but one that works well. It is also delicious with arugula instead of lettuce.

2 tablespoons lime juice
1 tablespoon water
¼ teaspoon sea salt
¼ teaspoon freshly ground black pepper
3 tablespoons canola oil
1 tablespoon minced fresh mint

½ medium cantaloupe, seeds removed
½ medium honeydew, seeds removed
1 medium wedge watermelon
¾ pound baby lettuces, washed and spun dry
    or arugula

Mix the lime juice, water, salt and pepper, canola oil, and mint in a small bowl. Taste for seasoning.

Use a melon baller to make balls from each kind of melon.

ASSEMBLY: Toss the lettuces with the lime dressing. Divide among 4 large salad plates. Garnish each salad with an assortment of melon balls.

LIME DRESSING
Calories 94;   Protein .25 g/1 cal;   Carbohydrates 1 g/4 cal;
Fat 10 g/89 cal;   (Saturated Fat 1 g/7 cal);   Cholesterol 0 mg;
Sodium 124 mg;   Fiber 0 g;   Vitamin C 9% of Daily Value

BABY HEAD LETTUCE WITH WATERMELON,
HONEYDEW, AND CANTALOUPE
Calories 70;   Protein 3 g/10 cal;   Carbohydrates 14 g/56 cal;
Fat .4 g/4 cal;   (Saturated Fat 0 g/0 cal);   Cholesterol 0 mg;
Sodium 19 mg;   Fiber 3 g;   Vitamin A 53% of Daily Value

MERINGUE WITH MANGO SORBET AND RASPBERRIES

❖ MERINGUE ❖

Meringues need to bake for 2 – 3 hours. If you have time, bake them the day before and store them in an airtight container.

Pinch sea salt
3 egg whites at room temperature
¾ cup superfine sugar

Add a pinch of salt to the egg whites and whip them by hand or in a mixer until they hold soft peaks. Add the sugar in a slow, steady stream while continuing to beat the egg whites. Once all the sugar is added, continue beating the egg whites until they look glossy and hold stiff peaks.

Preheat the oven to 225°F.

Line a 12 x 18-inch baking sheet with aluminum foil, shiny-side-down. Trace four, 4-inch circles in the foil. Put the meringue in a pastry bag fitted with a large star tip and pipe out 4 meringue baskets. Form the baskets by starting at the center of the traced circle and piping around and around to make the base. Pipe another 2 layers around the edge to make the sides higher than the center. You can also use a spoon to shape the baskets.

Bake the meringues for 2 – 3 hours or until dry. Meringue should be white. If the meringue baskets begin to color in the oven, lower the oven temperature and continue baking until they are completely dry.

At Nora's, I like to make desserts with egg whites since they contain no fat and no cholesterol.

My favorite childhood dessert was meringue. At Christmas, my mother decorated our tree with edible decorations, including meringue disks. After January 6th, the Feast of the Epiphany, when it was time to take down the tree, she didn't have many ornaments to remove—my sisters and I had eaten nearly everything!

✳ MANGO SORBET AND RASPBERRIES

You will need an ice cream maker.

3 mangoes (3½ pounds)
3 – 4 tablespoons sugar
½ cup orange juice

1 teaspoon lime juice
¼ cup rum or tequila

½ pint raspberries
Mint for garnish

Halve the mangoes, cutting around the large pit, and remove the pulp from the skin. Add the mango pulp, sugar, citrus juices, and rum to a blender. Purée until smooth. Refrigerate to cool. Freeze in an ice cream freezer according to manufacturer's directions.

ASSEMBLY: Arrange the meringue baskets on 4 dinner plates. Place a big scoop of sorbet in each one. Sprinkle the top and sides with raspberries. Garnish with mint.

The texture of the sorbet can be made lighter by adding some whipped egg whites to the fruit purée. You can also experiment and try making herb sorbets, using lavender, lemon balm, mint or tarragon instead of mangoes.

This mango purée is flavorful and versatile. Add more orange juice or water and you have a mango sauce to serve with chocolate cake, fresh berries, or chocolate sorbet. Add yogurt to the purée, freeze in an ice cream freezer, and you have mango frozen yogurt.

MERINGUE
Calories 156;   Protein 3 g/11 cal;   Carbohydrates 36 g/145 cal;
Fat 0 g/0 cal;   (Saturated Fat 0 g/0 cal);   Cholesterol 0 mg;
Sodium 46 mg;   Fiber 0 g

MANGO SORBET (1 OUNCE) AND RASPBERRIES
Calories 21;   Protein 0 g/0 cal;   Carbohydrates 5 g/20 cal;
Fat .1 g/1 cal;   (Saturated Fat 0 g/0 cal);   Cholesterol 0 mg;
Sodium 0 mg;   Fiber 1 g;   Vitamin C 13% of Daily Value

SUMMER MENU II

GRILLED SHRIMP WITH MANGO-AVOCADO RELISH AND WATERCRESS

TEN KINDS OF TOMATOES WITH FRESH BASIL AND BALSAMIC VINAIGRETTE

GRILLED, ROSEMARY-MARINATED NEW YORK STRIP STEAK WITH EGGPLANT-RED PEPPER RAGOUT

CHERRY CLAFOUTIS

WINE SELECTIONS

This menu is perfect for red wine. An elegant Bordeaux, preferably a Pomerol or a soft California Merlot, would make the best companion.

Havens Reserve Merlot 1989 Napa, California

Château Latour à Pomerol 1985, France

GRILLED SHRIMP WITH MANGO-AVOCADO RELISH AND WATERCRESS

MANGO-AVOCADO RELISH

1 large, ripe, soft mango
2 ripe and soft avocados (6 to 8 ounces each)
2 tablespoons lime juice

1 tablespoon minced cilantro or mint leaves
1 small chili pepper, minced (optional)
Sea salt and freshly ground black pepper

Halve the mango, cutting around each side of the large pit. Peel the halves and cut into ¼-inch cubes. Halve the avocados, remove the pit, peel, and cut the flesh into ¼-inch cubes. Mix the mango and avocado with the lime juice, cilantro or mint, optional chili, and salt and pepper to taste.

GRILLED SHRIMP

2 tablespoons lemon juice
1 tablespoon olive oil
1 teaspoon chopped garlic
Sea salt and freshly ground black pepper
1 pound medium shrimp, peeled, deveined

1 bunch watercress, stems trimmed, washed and spun dry, for garnish
4 bamboo skewers soaked in water for 15 minutes, or 4 metal skewers

Mix the lemon juice, olive oil, garlic, and salt and pepper in a medium bowl. Remove 1 tablespoon of the marinade and set aside. Put the shrimp into the bowl, toss to coat, and marinate for at least 15 minutes, preferably 1 hour.

Remove the shrimp from the marinade, and thread them evenly on 4 bamboo skewers. The skewers are easier to turn on the grill than the individual shrimp. Grill or broil 1 minute on each side or until opaque but just cooked through. Don't overcook or the shrimp will become rubbery and tough.

ASSEMBLY: Toss the watercress in the reserved marinade. Arrange the shrimp in a half circle on the plate. Place a spoonful of relish in the center. Garnish with a small bunch of watercress.

GRILLED SHRIMP
Calories 145; Protein 24 g/96 cal; Carbohydrates 2 g/7 cal;
Fat 5 g/42 cal; (Saturated Fat 1 g/7 cal); Cholesterol 221 mg;
Sodium 522 mg; Fiber 0 g; Iron 20% of Daily Value

MANGO-AVOCADO RELISH
Calories 208; Protein 2 g/9 cal; Carbohydrates 16 g/63 cal;
Fat 15 g/136 cal; (Saturated Fat 2 g/20 cal); Cholesterol 0 mg;
Sodium 76 mg; Fiber 4 g; Vitamin C 47% Daily Value

This relish makes a delicious quesadilla. Spread it between 2 flour tortillas, add a slice of brie or mozzarella, and bake until the cheese melts and the tortilla gets lightly brown. Cut into quarters and garnish with cilantro and lime wedges. Add fresh chopped jalapeño peppers for a spicy quesadilla.

In my opinion, relishes, salsas, and vinaigrettes are the sauces of the 90s. Healthier and lighter than traditional butter or cream sauces, they are also versatile. This same mango-avocado relish can be used as a sauce for grilled mushrooms or fish!

To peel and devein the shrimp at the same time, insert a small paring knife under the center of the curved back shell of the shrimp. As you lift the shell up and off the shrimp, use the tip of the knife to loosen the dark vein. Rinse the shrimp when finished.

Because watercress can be quite spicy on its own, taste it before deciding whether you want to add chili pepper.

Ten Kinds of Tomatoes with Fresh Basil and Balsamic Vinaigrette

Balsamic Vinaigrette ✳

In August and September, Cass Peterson of Flickerville Farm brings us wonderful organic tomatoes. We look forward to these tomatoes all year. In fact, this salad has become a signature dish at Nora's. This salad illustrates how the Petersons farm. They raise a wide variety of beautiful, unusual vegetables, and these tomatoes are just one glorious example.

To make a summer supper of this salad, toss it with hot pasta and add some cheese and black or green olives as a garnish. Delicious!

1 tablespoon balsamic vinegar
2 tablespoons olive oil

½ teaspoon chopped garlic
Sea salt and freshly ground black pepper

Pour the vinegar and salt into a small bowl, add the olive oil, garlic, and pepper and mix. Adjust seasonings to taste.

Ten Kinds of Tomatoes

10 kinds of tomatoes 1 - 1 ¼ pounds,
*   or an assortment such as:*
1 red tomato
1 yellow tomato
1 red cherry tomato
1 yellow cherry tomato
1 red pear tomato

1 yellow pear tomato
1 red currant tomato
1 yellow currant tomato
1 orange or yellow sunburst tomato
1 green grape tomato
1 cup basil leaves, cut into julienne
Basil leaves, for garnish

Wash and slice the large tomatoes, quarter the medium ones, and halve the small ones. Leave the currant tomatoes whole. Toss with the balsamic vinaigrette and the julienned basil leaves.

ASSEMBLY: Divide the tomatoes among 4 luncheon plates and garnish with whole basil leaves.

TEN KINDS OF TOMATOES
Calories 69;   Protein 2 g/9 cal;   Carbohydrates 13 g/52 cal;
Fat 1 g/8 cal;   (Saturated Fat .1 g/1 cal);   Cholesterol 0 mg;
Sodium 29 mg;   Fiber 3 g;
Vitamin A and Iron 38% of Daily Value

BALSAMIC VINAIGRETTE
Calories 68;   Protein .25 g/1 cal;   Carbohydrates 2 g/7 cal;
Fat 7 g/60 cal;   (Saturated Fat 1 g/9 cal);   Cholesterol 0 mg;
Sodium 85 mg;   Fiber 0 g;   Iron 2% of Daily Value

GRILLED, ROSEMARY-MARINATED NEW YORK STRIP STEAK WITH EGGPLANT-RED PEPPER RAGOUT

MARINATED NEW YORK STRIP STEAK ❖

Our beef comes from Garnett Farm in Virginia, raised for us by Steve Garnett. Organic meat is extremely lean and flavorful but tougher than what you might be accustomed to.

Soon after I came to this country, my former husband, Pierre, and I took a car trip west during which we lived on steak and baked potatoes. The further west we drove, the bigger the steaks and the baked potatoes became. After a while, the plates could hardly hold them. As recent arrivals from France, steak was the best and most affordable American luxury especially in the Midwest.

If you have leftovers, scramble some eggs with the eggplant ragout for a great breakfast or, for lunch, add slices of prosciutto or another cured ham.

You can also wrap the ragout in Greek filo dough with feta or goat cheese for a vegetarian strudel.

2 tablespoons tamari or soy sauce
1 tablespoon minced onion
2 tablespoons minced garlic
2 tablespoons olive oil
1 teaspoon minced rosemary

3-inch piece of ginger, peeled and minced
1 tablespoon Dijon mustard

4 New York strip steaks or other steak, about 8 ounces each

Combine the tamari, onion, garlic, olive oil, rosemary, ginger, and mustard in a medium bowl and whisk to blend.

Put the steaks in a glass or non-reactive baking dish and pour the marinade over them. Allow to marinate for at least 2 hours, but preferably overnight, in the refrigerator.

Preheat the grill or broiler.

Grill or broil the steaks for about 4 minutes on each side for medium rare, or until desired doneness.

EGGPLANT-RED PEPPER RAGOUT

1 medium onion, chopped
3 tablespoons olive oil
1 teaspoon minced garlic
1 1/2 pounds eggplant unpeeled, cut into 1-inch cubes
1/2 teaspoon sea salt
3/4 pound zucchini, sliced into 1/2-inch rounds

3 medium red or yellow peppers, cut into 1-inch pieces
1/4 cup chopped, mixed fresh herbs such as thyme, oregano, and parsley
2 tablespoons balsamic vinegar
Freshly ground black pepper
Bouquet of fresh herbs for garnish

Sauté the onion in olive oil in a large sauté pan for 3 – 4 minutes or until soft. Add the garlic and eggplant and, stirring to combine, coat with the oil. Season with salt to release the juices of the eggplant.

Sauté until the eggplant gets soft, about 5 minutes, stirring from time to time. Add the zucchini, stir, and sauté for 2 – 3 minutes. Add the peppers and mixed herbs and sauté for another 3 – 5 minutes. Add the balsamic vinegar, and adjust the seasoning to taste.

Remove the ragout from the heat when the peppers are nearly tender. The heat of the pan will finish cooking them. Cool to room temperature.

ASSEMBLY: Put one steak on each of 4 dinner plates. Mound a generous serving of eggplant ragout next to it. Garnish with a bouquet of fresh herbs.

EGGPLANT-RED PEPPER RAGOUT
Calories 127;   Protein 3 g/10 cal;   Carbohydrates 8 g/32 cal;
Fat 9 g/85 cal;   (Saturated Fat 1 g/13 cal);   Cholesterol 0 mg;
Sodium 74 mg;   Fiber 4 g;   Iron 20% of Daily Value

NEW YORK STRIP STEAK
Calories 399;   Protein 54 g/214 cal;   Carbohydrates 4 g/15 cal;
Fat 19 g/170 cal;   (Saturated Fat 6 g/52 cal);   Cholesterol 109 mg;
Sodium 228 mg;   Fiber 0 g;   Iron 26% of Daily Value

CHERRY CLAFOUTIS

Traditionally, the cherry pits are left in a clafoutis, but you should do as you like. In Austria, my grandmother used to make this dessert, called Kirschenkuchen. We children loved to have contests to see who could spit the cherry pits the farthest.

You can also substitute pitted apricots, prunes, or plums for the cherries.

4 cups (2 pints) black cherries, pitted (optional)
⅓ cup kirsch
1 teaspoon butter
5 eggs
⅓ cup sugar
1 teaspoon grated lemon peel

Pinch of salt
1 teaspoon vanilla
2 cups milk
⅓ cup unbleached flour
Confectioner's sugar for garnish
Light whipped cream (page 53)

Preheat the oven to 325° F.

Put the cherries into a medium bowl and pour the kirsch over them, stirring to blend. Set aside for at least 30 minutes to marinate. Butter a 10-inch baking dish and dust with some of the sugar.

Combine the eggs and sugar in the bowl of an electric mixer and beat until frothy. Add the grated lemon peel, salt, and vanilla. Slowly pour in the milk, beating until the batter is smooth. Use a strainer to sift in the flour, continuing to beat, until the batter is smooth.

Pour half of the batter into the baking dish, add the cherries, and cover with the remaining batter. Bake for 50 minutes or until the batter is firm and the top is golden. Sprinkle with confectioner's sugar and eat while still warm.

ASSEMBLY: Spoon 4 portions of the clafoutis onto luncheon plates. Garnish with a generous dollop of light whipped cream. Serve warm.

CHERRY CLAFOUTIS
Calories 211;   Protein 7 g/29 cal;   Carbohydrates 32 g/126 cal;
Fat 6 g/56 cal;   (Saturated Fat 3 g/25 cal);   Cholesterol 143 mg;
Sodium 146 mg;   Fiber 1 g;   Calcium 10% of Daily Value

SUMMER MENU III

Cold Cucumber Soup with Garlic and Cilantro

Arugula, Red and Yellow Cherry Tomato Salad with Black Olives and
Tamari-Balsamic Vinaigrette

Grilled Swordfish with Avocado-Lime Salsa, Grilled Tomato, Corn On The Cob, and Kale

Russian Blueberry and Raspberry Pudding

WINE SELECTIONS

*Swordfish goes well with so many wines, it is a true wine lover's fish. A red Pinot Noir from California or a white
Chassagne Montrachet from France will stand up to the firmness of this wonderful fish.*

Chassagne Montrachet 1989 Bernard Morey

Morgan Pinot Noir 1990 Monterey California

COLD CUCUMBER SOUP WITH GARLIC AND CILANTRO*

3 cups low-fat yogurt

3 medium cucumbers, peeled, seeded, and cut into chunks

1 medium green pepper, washed, seeded, and cut into chunks

4 – 6 cloves of garlic, peeled

Juice of 1 lemon

Peel of 1 lemon

1 tablespoon olive oil

1/3 cup cilantro leaves

1 jalapeño chili pepper with seeds, stemmed

1 teaspoon sea salt

Cilantro sprigs, for garnish

Put the yogurt, cucumbers, green pepper, garlic, lemon juice and lemon peel, olive oil, cilantro, and jalapeño in a blender. Purée until smooth. Season to taste with salt and refrigerate.

ASSEMBLY: Pour the chilled soup into 4 bowls, garnish with cilantro.

CUCUMBER SOUP
Calories 128;   Protein 8 g/32 cal;   Carbohydrates 17 g/66 cal;
Fat 3 g/30 cal;   (Saturated Fat 1 g/10 cal);   Cholesterol 5 mg;
Sodium 376 mg;   Fiber 3 g;   Calcium 21% of Daily Value

Since the fruit I use is organic, I always use the skins. I zest or peel my lemons or limes with a vegetable peeler. Then I peel off the white pith from the fruit (you need a sharp paring knife) and put the whole lemon or lime and its peeled skin into the blender.

Be sure to add enough salt. Cucumbers and yogurt need a lot of salt.

ARUGULA, RED AND YELLOW CHERRY TOMATO SALAD WITH BLACK OLIVES AND TAMARI-BALSAMIC VINAIGRETTE

TAMARI-BALSAMIC VINAIGRETTE*

1 tablespoon balsamic vinegar

1 teaspoon tamari

2 cloves garlic, finely minced

1/4 teaspoon of freshly ground black pepper

2 tablespoons olive oil

Put the vinegar, tamari, garlic, and pepper in a small bowl and whisk with a fork. Add the olive oil slowly, stirring until blended.

Visiting Modena on a recent trip to Italy, I went to a store that sold aged vinegar. The shopkeeper told me that balsamic vinegar is such a part of their culture that when a Modena woman marries, she gets a small flask of 100-year-old balsamic vinegar so she can start her own vintages.

I often use tamari or Bragg's amino acid instead of salt. But be careful not to overdue it— both are salty and strong in flavor. Use light tamari or soy sauce if you want the flavor without the sodium.

Arugula, "roquette" in French, has recently become popular in the U.S. It is peppery and easy to grow. We grow it in our herb garden in front of the restaurant nearly year round.

¹/₂ pound arugula, trimmed, washed and spun dry

¹/₂ pound red cherry tomatoes

¹/₂ pound yellow cherry tomatoes

20 black olives, oil or dry-cured, Greek or Moroccan

Tamari-balsamic vinaigrette

Cut the cherry tomatoes in half. Toss them with the arugula and the tamari-balsamic vinaigrette.

ASSEMBLY: Divide the salad among 4 luncheon plates and top with black olives.

ARUGULA, RED AND YELLOW CHERRY
TOMATO SALAD
Calories 40;   Protein 2 g/8 cal;   Carbohydrates 6 g/25 cal;
Fat 1 g/7 cal;   (Saturated Fat .1 g/1 cal);   Cholesterol 0 mg;
Sodium 84 mg;   Fiber 2 g;   Vitamin C 58% of Daily Value

TAMARI VINAIGRETTE
Calories 68;   Protein .25 g/1 cal;   Carbohydrates 2 g/7 cal;
Fat 7 g/60 cal;   (Saturated Fat 1 g/9 cal);   Cholesterol 0 mg;
Sodium 85 mg;   Fiber 0 g;   Iron 2% of Daily Value

GRILLED SWORDFISH WITH AVOCADO-LIME SALSA, GRILLED TOMATO, CORN ON THE COB, AND KALE

AVOCADO-LIME SALSA

1 large ripe avocado
1 lime
³/₄ – 1 cup water
¹/₂ teaspoon cumin
¹/₃ cup cilantro, packed loosely

¹/₂ jalapeño chili pepper with seeds
4 cloves of garlic
¹/₂ teaspoon sea salt or to taste
Freshly ground black pepper

Cut the avocado in half. Remove the seed and scoop out the pulp with a tablespoon and put into the blender.

Peel the skin of the lime with a vegetable peeler. Remove the pith from the peeled lime and discard it. Cut the flesh into quarters and put it and the lime peel into a blender. Add ¾ cup of the water, cumin, cilantro, chili, garlic, and salt and pepper. Purée until smooth. If the salsa is too thick, add the remaining water to thin it out.

The salsa should be both spicy and tart to cut the richness of the avocado and swordfish. This salsa also makes a good dip with tortilla chips or raw vegetables. Add chopped tomatoes and onion and you have guacamole.

I often use the zest of citrus fruit to add flavor to marinades and vinaigrettes.

4 swordfish steaks, 6 ounces each
2 teaspoons olive oil

Sea salt and freshly ground black pepper

Heat the grill or broiler.

Brush the swordfish with olive oil and season with salt and pepper to taste. Grill or broil the swordfish 4 – 5 minutes on each side for medium.

GRILLED TOMATO, CORN ON THE COB, AND KALE

2 tomatoes, cut in half
Olive oil for brushing the tomatoes
Sea salt and freshly ground black pepper

2 ears of corn, husks and silks removed, cut or broken into halves
½ pound kale, washed, cut into pieces, and large stems removed

Brush the tomatoes with olive oil and season to taste with salt and pepper. Grill or broil for 3 minutes on each side or until cooked through and marked by the grill.

Fill a medium saucepan ¾ with water and bring it to a boil. Add the corn and cook for 3 – 5 minutes or until tender. Remove the corn from the water with tongs and don't pour out the water.

Use the same water to cook the kale. Bring it back to a boil and add the kale. Cook for 1 – 2 minutes, until the color turns bright green and the leaves start to wilt. Drain, but leave some water on the leaves. Season lightly with olive oil, salt, and pepper to taste.

ASSEMBLY: Put the swordfish on a dinner plate. Top with the avocado salsa. Arrange the grilled tomato, corn, and kale around the swordfish.

GRILLED TOMATO, CORN ON THE COB, AND KALE
Calories 83;   Protein 3 g/12 cal;   Carbohydrates 16 g/63 cal;
Fat 1 g/8 cal;   (Saturated Fat .1 g/1 cal);   Cholesterol 0 mg;
Sodium 204 mg;   Fiber 3 g;   Calcium 10% of Daily Value

AVOCADO-LIME SALSA
Calories 88;   Protein 2 g/8 cal;   Carbohydrates 4 g/16 cal;
Fat 7 g/64 cal;   (Saturated Fat 0 g/0 cal);   Cholesterol 0 mg;
Sodium 326 mg;   Fiber 7 g;   Vitamin C 67% of Daily Valu

GRILLED SWORDFISH
Calories 218;   Protein 34 g/135 cal;   Carbohydrates .25 g/1 cal;
Fat 9 g/82 cal;   (Saturated Fat 2 g/20 cal);   Cholesterol 67 mg;
Sodium 286 mg;   Fiber 0 g;   Iron 9% of Daily Value

Swordfish is caught off the coast of New England in summer and fall. At Nora's, we buy a 80–100 pound fish from the coldest water available and cut it up ourselves. The freshness of the fish is easier to judge when you buy it whole. With swordfish trimmings, we make Asian stir-fries or Middle Eastern kebabs.

This recipe also works well with tuna or Mako shark.

Grilled tomatoes spread with tapenade, a black olive paste from Provence, make a great appetizer.

It is nice to have little food on big plates. At Nora's we serve both appetizer and main courses on oversized plates, and salads and desserts on dinner plates. Steven and I were traveling in France when I discovered big plates and how beautiful the food looked when set against a large, white surface.

RUSSIAN BLUEBERRY AND RASPBERRY PUDDING

1 pint blueberries, washed and drained
1 pint raspberries, washed and drained
1 cup low-fat yogurt

¼ cup brown sugar
Fresh mint for garnish

Preheat the broiler.

Divide berries among 4 individual oven-proof dishes. Top each with ¼ of the yogurt and sprinkle with 1 tablespoon of brown sugar. Broil for 3   5 minutes or until the sugar melts and caramelizes on the top. Garnish with mint.

RUSSIAN BLUEBERRY AND RASPBERRY PUDDING
Calories 169;   Protein 4 g/16 cal;   Carbohydrates 35 g/139 cal;
Fat 2 g/14 cal;   (Saturated Fat .6 g/5 cal);   Cholesterol 4 mg;
Sodium 48 mg;   Fiber 5 g;   Vitamin C 45% of Daily Value

The original recipe calls for sour cream rather than yogurt. Perhaps this is why it is called Russian Pudding. I keep the name even though my version lacks many of the calories of the original!

For a variation, put a single layer of grapes on a plate and cover them with a layer of yogurt or sour cream. Sprinkle heavily with dark brown sugar and leave to marinate for a few hours. The brown sugar seeps through to create a delicious cream.

SUMMER MENU IV

Jewell Yam Vichyssoise with Chive Flowers

Artichoke with Fresh Goat Cheese and Corn Relish, Black Olive Vinaigrette

Grilled Lemon-Marinated Chicken Breast with
Egyptian Eggplant-Roasted Red Pepper Salad and Batvia Lettuce

Peaches in Red Wine with Mint

WINE SELECTIONS

A crisp dry white wine such as a Sauvignon Blanc from
California or a Graves from Bordeaux will work with the delicate chicken breast.
Chateau Graville Lacoste 1990 Graves
Long Sauvignon Blanc 1991 Napa, California

JEWELL YAM VICHYSSOISE WITH CHIVE FLOWERS

2 tablespoons canola oil
1 medium onion, peeled and coarsely chopped
1 leek, white part only, washed and sliced
1 pound Jewell yams, butternut squash, or
    sweet potatoes, peeled and cut into
    ½-inch slices

2 cups chicken or vegetable stock
1 cup whole milk
Sea salt and freshly ground pepper
⅛ teaspoon mace or nutmeg or to taste
Chive flowers and chopped chives for garnish

Heat the canola oil in a large saucepan. Add the onions and leeks and sauté on a medium flame, stirring from time to time, until brown, about 15 minutes. Add the yams, squash, or sweet potatoes, the chicken or vegetable stock, and stir to combine.

Bring to a boil, cover, reduce the heat, and simmer for 30 minutes or until the yams are tender. Remove from the stove and add the milk to the saucepan, stirring to combine. Purée the soup in small batches — there will be too much to fit into the blender or food processor at once. Season to taste with salt and pepper and mace or nutmeg.

Refrigerate for at least 1 hour to chill.

Assembly: Divide the soup among 4 chilled soup bowls. Garnish with minced chives and chive blossoms. Serve chilled.

JEWELL YAM VICHYSSOISE WITH CHIVE FLOWERS
Calories 265;   Protein 5 g/18 cal;   Carbohydrates 41 g/163 cal;
Fat 9 g/84 cal;   (Saturated Fat 2 g/16 cal);   Cholesterol 8 mg;
Sodium 283 mg;   Fiber 4 g;   Calcium 14% of Daily Value

Serve this soup hot in the winter as Yam and Leek soup, changing the garnish to croutons (page 190) or chopped chives.

I like to use Jewell yams because they are not as sweet as some other varieties and have a beautiful color.

Yams and sweet potatoes are not from the same botanical family, but they are very similar in taste. Yams and sweet potatoes are tubers. Yams are from Asia and are higher in calories and carbohydrates than sweet potatoes. They can grow to be enormous, over 3 feet long. Sweet potatoes have their origin in the Americas and are nearer the size of baking potatoes.

ARTICHOKE WITH FRESH GOAT CHEESE AND CORN RELISH, BLACK OLIVE VINAIGRETTE

BLACK OLIVE VINAIGRETTE *

½ cup black olives, preferably Kalamata,
    pitted and finely chopped
1 tablespoon red wine vinegar
1 teaspoon fresh thyme leaves

½ teaspoon garlic, minced
1 teaspoon shallots, minced
4 tablespoons olive oil
Sea salt and freshly ground black pepper

Mix the olives, vinegar, thyme, garlic, and shallots in a medium bowl, add the olive oil, and stir to combine. Season to taste with salt and pepper.

To prepare the olives quickly, put them on a cutting board and cover with a paper towel. Press down with the flat side of a large knife until you crush the olives. Now you can easily squeeze out the pits.

Black olive vinaigrette is also good with an arugula, tomato, and feta cheese salad.

This corn-red pepper relish is versatile. Use it as an appetizer with grilled eggplant or grilled portobello mushrooms, or as a main course with grilled pork chops or tuna. I sometimes sprinkle it over a green salad.

2 ears corn, husk and silks removed
1 large red pepper, washed, seeded, and cut into ¼-inch dice
1 – 2 green onions, washed, trimmed, and thinly sliced (about 3 tablespoons) or 3 tablespoons minced chives

2 tablespoons chopped flat leaf parsley
Sea salt and freshly ground black pepper
1 tablespoon olive oil

Cut the corn from the cob and put it in a medium bowl. Add the red pepper, green onions or chives, and parsley. Stir to combine and season to taste with salt and pepper.

Heat olive oil in a small pan, add the vegetable mixture, and sauté for 1 – 2 minutes, just until the corn looses its raw taste. If your corn is very fresh, sweet, and tender, this step is not necessary. Just add the olive oil to the raw vegetables and stir to combine.

4 large artichokes, about 2½ pounds
½ lemon, sliced
1 tablespoon of dried bouquet garni including
    6 black peppercorns, wrapped in a piece
    of cheesecloth (optional)

4 ounces goat cheese such as Montrachet, sliced
    into 4 rounds

If you want to serve only the artichoke, leave it whole but remove the choke. Purée the black olive vinaigrette so it will be thick enough to cling to the leaves, and pour it into the center of the artichoke.

Bouquet Garni is a mixture of herbs such as thyme, bay leaf, celery seeds, and parsley. Fines Herbes is a mixture of chervil, chives, tarragon, and parsley.

Trim the base of the artichoke so that it sits flat. Trim the leaves with scissors to remove spines. Cut off the top ⅓ of each artichoke and discard. Bring a large saucepan of water to a boil. Add the lemon slices, the optional bouquet garni, and the artichokes. Weight the artichokes with a plate or heavy lid, so that they stay below the surface of the water.

Simmer the artichokes for 45 – 60 minutes, until tender and a central leaf pulls out easily. Remove the artichokes and drain them upside down. Set aside to cool.

ASSEMBLY: Pull off the artichoke leaves, and arrange in a circle on a dinner plate, overlapping the leaves. Remove the hairy choke with a teaspoon or paring knife and put the artichoke bottom in the center of the circle of leaves. Top with a slice of goat cheese and the corn relish. Dress with the black olive vinaigrette.

ARTICHOKES WITH FRESH GOAT CHEESE
Calories 159;   Protein 9 g/35 cal;   Carbohydrates 15 g/60 cal;
Fat 7 g/64 cal;   (Saturated Fat 4 g/39 cal);   Cholesterol 25 mg;
Sodium 280 mg;   Fiber 5 g;   Iron 15% of Daily Value

BLACK OLIVE DRESSING
Calories 145;   Protein .5 g/2 cal;   Carbohydrates .25 g/1 cal;
Fat 16 g/142 cal;   (Saturated Fat 2 g/20 cal);   Cholesterol 0 mg;
Sodium 68 mg;   Fiber 1 g;   Iron 6% of Daily Value

CORN RELISH
Calories 95;   Protein 2 g/7 cal;   Carbohydrates 15 g/58 cal;
Fat 3 g/30 cal;   (Saturated Fat 0 g/0 cal);   Cholesterol 0 mg;
Sodium 270 mg;   Fiber 2 g;   Vitamin C 38% of Daily Value

Grilled Lemon-Marinated Chicken Breast with Egyptian Eggplant-Roasted Red Pepper Salad and French Batavia Lettuce

This dish is easy to prepare, especially if you have a stove-top grill. Make the marinade and pour it over the chicken while you make dinner one evening, and cook the chicken and vegetables the following night.

This is a classic Mediterranean marinade which also works well with tuna or swordfish.

2 tablespoons lemon juice

4 garlic cloves, minced

2 tablespoons olive oil

2 tablespoons minced tarragon or 1 tablespoon minced rosemary

¼ teaspoon ground cumin

Sea salt and freshly ground black pepper

4 boneless chicken breasts, 8 – 10 ounces each

Preheat the grill or broiler.

Mix the lemon juice, garlic, olive oil, tarragon or rosemary, salt, and pepper together in a small bowl.

Put the chicken breasts in a glass or non-reactive dish and pour the marinade over them. Refrigerate and allow to marinate at least 2 hours, preferably overnight.

Grill or broil the chicken breasts for about 5 minutes, skin-side-down, then turn and cook for 4 minutes on the other side or until cooked through.

This eggplant salad makes a nice appetizer, garnished with arugula, yogurt, and some black olives. I also like to serve this salad on a thick slice of toasted garlic bread, like Italian bruschetta.

Batavia is a baby head lettuce that is a cross between leaf and Bibb lettuce.

To grill the peppers quickly over an open gas flame, put them directly on the burner and turn them with tongs so they blister and char. Remove them when skin is completely charred and proceed with the recipe.

You can substitute 4 tomatoes, seeded and cubed, for the peppers. Add some feta cheese to this salad and serve it on top of cooked fettuccine for a Mediterranean pasta dish.

3 tablespoons olive oil
1 tablespoon tamari
2 tablespoons balsamic vinegar
3 teaspoons minced garlic
$\frac{1}{2}$ teaspoon raz el hanout or a pinch each of cardamom, mace, allspice, ginger, and cinnamon.
Sea salt and freshly ground black pepper

1 large eggplant (about 1 to 1 $\frac{1}{4}$ pounds), cut into $\frac{1}{2}$-inch slices
2 large red sweet peppers
3 tablespoons chopped basil or cilantro

2 heads Batavia or similar lettuce, washed, spun dry, and separated into leaves
Bouquet of fresh herbs for garnish

Preheat the grill or broiler.

Make a vinaigrette with the olive oil, tamari, vinegar, garlic, raz el hanout or other spices. Season to taste with salt and pepper.

Brush the eggplant slices with some of the vinaigrette. Grill or broil the eggplant on each side for 2 minutes or until tender. Cool and cut into strips or $\frac{1}{2}$-inch cubes.

Grill or broil peppers, turning until all the skin blisters and chars. Put peppers into a bowl, seal with plastic wrap, and allow to steam for 6 – 8 minutes.

When the peppers are cool enough to handle, peel off the charred outer skin and seed them. Rinse the peppers quickly under running water, if necessary. Cut them into strips or squares.

Put the peppers, eggplant, and basil or cilantro into a medium bowl and pour the remaining vinaigrette over them. Toss to coat.

ASSEMBLY: Divide the Batavia lettuce among 4 dinner plates. Top with the grilled chicken breast and add a big spoon of eggplant and red pepper salad on the side. Serve warm or at room temperature.

LEMON-MARINATED CHICKEN BREAST
Calories 367;   Protein 57 g/229 cal;   Carbohydrates 3 g/10 cal;
Fat 14 g/128 cal;   (Saturated Fat 3 g/28 cal);   Cholesterol 154 mg;
Sodium 137 mg;   Fiber 0 g;   Iron 15% of Daily Value

EGGPLANT AND ROASTED RED PEPPER SALAD
Calories 161;   Protein 3 g/13 cal;   Carbohydrates 16 g/62 cal;
Fat 10 g/86 cal;   (Saturated Fat 2 g/14 cal);   Cholesterol 0 mg;
Sodium 262 mg;   Fiber 5 g;   Iron 14% of Daily Value

PEACHES IN RED WINE WITH MINT

3 cups fruity red wine, such as Zinfandel or
    Beaujolais
2 − 3 tablespoons sugar

6 − 8 (1½ pounds) medium peaches
Fresh mint for garnish

Pour the wine into a medium bowl and add the sugar to taste, depending upon the sweetness of the wine and the peaches. Stir to dissolve the sugar.

    Cut the peaches in half, pit them, and slice into wedges or quarters.

    ASSEMBLY: Divide the peaches among 4 wine glasses. Pour the sweetened wine over the peaches. Refrigerate, allowing the peaches to marinate for ½ hour. Garnish with a sprig of mint.

PEACHES IN RED WINE
Calories 120;   Protein 2 g/7 cal;   Carbohydrates 28 g/112 cal;
Fat .1 g/1 cal;   (Saturated Fat 0 g/0 cal);   Cholesterol 0 mg;
Sodium 92 mg;   Fiber 3 g;   Vitamin C 18% of Daily Value

Peaches in red wine is a traditional dessert from the south of France and Italy. My French husband used to make it for us when peaches were in season. Steven, my partner, tells me that his Sicilian grandfather, who came to the United States as a stowaway, often made this dessert using the peaches from his own peach trees.

SUMMER MENU V

WATERMELON GAZPACHO WITH LIME AND MINT

GRILLED SUMMER VEGETABLES WITH HUMMUS

SAUTÉED SOFT-SHELL CRABS WITH CILANTRO VINAIGRETTE AND SAFFRON FETTUCCINE
WITH TOMATO-GREEN ONION SALAD

BLACKBERRY COBBLER

WINE SELECTIONS

This menu calls for a full-bodied California Chardonnay or a rich Meursault to balance the excitement of the cilantro vinaigrette.

Kistler McCrea 1990 Sonoma California

Meursault Blagny 1991 Joseph Matrot

WATERMELON GAZPACHO WITH LIME AND MINT*

6 pounds watermelon
2 tablespoons lime juice
2 tablespoons lemon juice
1 whole red chili pepper
½ cup sliced red onion
2 garlic cloves, minced

⅓ cup minced mint
1 zucchini, seeded and cut in ¼-inch dice
1 green pepper, seeded and cut in ¼-inch dice
Sea salt and freshly ground black pepper
Fresh mint for garnish

Gazpacho is a very refreshing soup, perfect when the weather is hot. You can make it with all kinds of melons. The original Spanish gazpacho is made with red tomatoes, seasoned with vinegar and olive oil, and garnished with diced vegetables and croutons.

Cut the watermelon into wedges and peel and seed them. Put the watermelon pieces into the blender, in batches, puréeing until smooth.

Pass the purée through a colander or a sieve to remove any remaining seeds. Pour half of the purée into a large bowl and the other half back into the blender. Add the lime and lemon juice, chili, onion, and garlic, and purée until smooth.

Pour this seasoned purée into the bowl with the reserved purée and stir in the mint, zucchini, and pepper. Season to taste with salt and pepper. Refrigerate.

ASSEMBLY: Divide the soup among 4 bowls. Garnish with mint. Serve chilled.

WATERMELON GAZPACHO WITH LIME AND MINT
Calories 235;   Protein 6 g/24 cal;   Carbohydrates 46 g/182 cal;
Fat 3 g/29 cal;   (Saturated Fat 0 g/0 cal);   Cholesterol 0 mg;
Sodium 286 mg;   Fiber 5 g;   Vitamin A 46% of Daily Value

GRILLED SUMMER VEGETABLES WITH HUMMUS

HUMMUS*

Soak the chick-peas overnight, if possible.

1½ cups dry chick-peas or 2 cups cooked and
    drained chick-peas
1 cup water
1 onion, peeled and coarsely chopped
3 tablespoons tahini, a Middle Eastern sesame
    paste available at specialty stores

6 cloves garlic
6 tablespoons lemon juice
1 teaspoon ground cumin
⅓ cup yogurt
1 tablespoon olive oil
Sea salt and freshly ground black pepper
3 tablespoons minced flat leaf parsley

If you don't presoak dry chick-peas, they take at least 1½ hours to cook before they are tender.

It is nice to have hummus ready in the refrigerator, so I often make more than called for in a recipe. It is a convenient and fast dip to serve with pita bread or raw vegetables, or on a toma-to sandwich made with pita, feta cheese, and arugula. Hummus is also great as a sauce for grilled lamb.

If using dry chick-peas, soak them overnight, pour off the water, and put them into a medium saucepan. Cover the peas with water, add the onion, and simmer for 1 hour or more until tender, adding more water as needed. If you are using cooked or canned chick-peas, this step is not necessary.

Drain the chick-peas and put them in a blender with the tahini, garlic, lemon juice, cumin, yogurt, and olive oil. Purée until smooth. Dilute purée with water if too thick. Season to taste with salt and pepper. Stir in minced parsley.

1 tablespoon balsamic vinegar

1 tablespoon tamari

2 tablespoons olive oil

2 teaspoons minced garlic

⅛ teaspoon freshly ground black pepper

2 carrots, peeled and cut in half lengthwise or in quarters, if large

4 leeks, white part only, washed and cut in half lengthwise

4 small yellow patty pan squash, cut into halves

1 large eggplant, cut into eight, ½-inch thick, round slices

2 red peppers, quartered and seeded

2 zucchinis, quartered

8 – 12 shiitake mushrooms, stems removed

Small bouquet of fresh herbs, such as parsley or thyme, for garnish

You can grill all kinds of vegetables and stove-top grills are very handy for quickly preparing both vegetables and meats.

Grilled vegetables make a great ratatouille with the addition of chopped fresh basil, grilled tomatoes, and some of the marinade. Or use them to make a vegetarian pizza—add a few slices of fresh mozzarella and a sprinkle of Parmesan to the vegetables and run the pizza under the broiler to melt the cheese.

To make the marinade, put the vinegar, tamari, olive oil, garlic, and black pepper into a small bowl and stir to combine.

Preheat the grill or broiler.

Brush the vegetables well with the marinade and spread them out on the grill or a baking sheet. Grill or broil them for 2 – 3 minutes on each side, until cooked through but still firm.

ASSEMBLY: Divide the grilled vegetables among 4 luncheon plates. Add a spoonful of hummus to each plate and garnish with the fresh herbs.

HUMMUS
Calories 300; Protein 12 g/47 cal; Carbohydrates 30 g/120 cal;
Fat 15 g/133 cal; (Saturated Fat 4 g/32 cal); Cholesterol 6 mg;
Sodium 283 mg; Fiber 7 g; Calcium 15% of Daily Value

BALSAMIC-TAMARI MARINADE
Calories 71; Protein 1 g/3 cal; Carbohydrates 2 g/9 cal;
Fat 7 g/59 cal; (Saturated Fat 1 g/9 cal); Cholesterol 0 mg;
Sodium 252 mg; Fiber 0 g; Iron 2% of Daily Value

GRILLED SUMMER VEGETABLES
Calories 198; Protein 7 g/28 cal; Carbohydrates 41 g/162 cal;
Fat 1 g/8 cal; (Saturated Fat .25 g/1 cal); Cholesterol 0 mg;
Sodium 60 mg; Fiber 8 g; Vitamin A 143% of Daily Value

SAUTÉED SOFT-SHELL CRABS WITH
CILANTRO VINAIGRETTE AND SAFFRON FETTUCCINE WITH
TOMATO-GREEN ONION SALAD

TOMATO-GREEN ONION SALAD

If the tomatoes are not sweet and ripe, add a little sugar.

For a summery salad, substitute basil for parsley. I do not use basil here because this menu pairs the salad with cilantro-flavored soft-shell crabs, and you don't want such strong, constrasting flavors in the same menu.

4 large tomatoes (2 pounds), cut in half
   and seeded
1 bunch green onions, trimmed
1 cup chopped flat leaf parsley

2 tablespoons olive oil
1 tablespoon balsamic vinegar
Sea salt and freshly ground black pepper

Cut the tomatoes into ¼-inch cubes using a serrated knife to facilitate the slicing of the tomato skin. Chop the green onions. Put the tomatoes, onions, and parsley together in a medium bowl. Add the olive oil and vinegar and season to taste with the salt and pepper. Toss to combine. Let marinate for at least 10 minutes.

You will need a pasta machine.

1 1/2 cups unbleached flour
3/4 cup semolina flour

3 eggs
1/4 teaspoon powdered saffron
1 teaspoon sea salt
1 tablespoon olive oil

Combine the flours on a work surface and make a well in the center. Break the eggs into the well, add the saffron, salt, and olive oil, and beat with a fork until combined. Gradually mix in the flour, working around the inside of the well, until most of the flour mixes into a ball of dough. Gather the dough together and knead it for 10 minutes or until pliable and smooth. Dust with flour from time to time if it becomes too sticky. You can also make the pasta in a food processor or in a mixer fitted with a dough hook.

Cut the dough into 8 pieces and shape it into flat ovals. Lightly dust the ovals with flour to prevent them from sticking. Also dust the pasta machine rollers. Pass the dough through the widest setting on the pasta machine (#1) about 10 times, folding it in half each time. The dough will become smooth and pliable.

Continue passing the dough through the machine, narrowing the setting each time, until the dough stretches to the desired thickness of about 1/16 of an inch for fettuccine noodles. Repeat the process until all of the dough is stretched.

Cut the pasta sheets into fettuccine noodles using the specified cutter. Sprinkle the pasta with flour or cornmeal to prevent it from sticking.

Bring a large pot of water to boil. Just before cooking the fettuccine, add 1/2 tablespoon of olive oil to the water to help prevent the pasta from sticking together. Add the fettuccine and boil for 3 – 4 minutes, until al dente. Drain. Toss with the fresh tomato-green onion salad.

If you don't have a pasta machine, you can roll and stretch the dough with a rolling pin until nearly transparent. These days, you can even buy good-quality, fresh pasta quite easily.

The first time I heard of serving hot pasta with cold tomato salad was in the late sixties in a James Beard recipe. He called it Spaghetti Estivi. When I made it for the first time, I thought it was the best thing I had ever eaten. To make this a main course pasta, add some grilled shrimp, diced cooked chicken, or fresh mozzarella.

CILANTRO VINAIGRETTE *

1 bunch cilantro, about 2 cups
4 cloves garlic, peeled
1 tablespoon Dijon mustard
2-inch piece ginger, peeled and thinly sliced across the fiber

1/2 cup water
2 tablespoons lime juice
1/2 green chili with seeds
1/2 cup canola oil
Sea salt and freshly ground black pepper

Put the cilantro, garlic, mustard, ginger, water, lime juice, and chili into a blender. Purée until smooth. With the motor running, remove the center of the blender top and pour in the oil in a thin stream. Blend until emulsified. Season to taste with salt and pepper.

This cilantro vinaigrette differs from the earlier recipe on page 22 because it is thickened with mustard instead of roasted shallots and garlic. The mustard also makes the vinaigrette emulsify. This vinaigrette goes well with pasta or even as a marinade or sauce for chicken, lamb, or fish.

Small soft-shell crabs are good stir-fried with bok choy, shiitakes, green onions, peppers, and a ginger-tamari sauce.

Soft-shell crabs, "soft crabs" as they are known on the Maryland's Eastern Shore, are Atlantic Blue Crabs that have just shed their shells. Watermen call crabs that are ready to shed "peelers," and watch them until they begin to back out of their old shells. Once peeled, the crabs are left in water for 2 hours to harden slightly. They are then removed and packed in trays lined with sea grass. As soon as the crabs leave the water, the hardening of the shells stops. If the crabs are left in water after shedding, their shells will completely harden in about 48 hours.

8 jumbo or 12 prime soft-shell crabs, preferably alive

2 – 3 tablespoons canola oil
4 sprigs of cilantro for garnish

Clean the soft crabs by cutting off the eyes and mouth with a pair of scissors. Lift the shell apron on the bottom and remove. Lift the points of the top shell and fold back. Cut off the gills and discard. Dry the crabs on paper towels.

Heat the oil in 2 large sauté pans, large enough to hold all the crabs. Put the crabs into the hot oil, top-side-down and sauté for 2 – 3 minutes, until they are crispy and the shells turn reddish. Turn the crabs—carefully so they do not lose their legs and claws—and cook on the other side for 2 – 3 minutes.

ASSEMBLY: Pour a pool of the cilantro vinaigrette onto one side of a large dinner plate. On the other side, pile the pasta dressed with the tomato-green onion salad. Arrange the crabs on the pool of vinaigrette, leaning them against the pasta. Garnish with sprigs of cilantro.

TOMATO-GREEN ONION SALAD
Calories 112; Protein 3 g/10 cal; Carbohydrates 13 g/53 cal; Fat 5 g/49 cal; (Saturated Fat 1 g/10 cal); Cholesterol 0 mg; Sodium 134 mg; Fiber 4 g; Vitamin C 105% of Daily Value

CILANTRO VINAIGRETTE
Calories 150; Protein 2 g/8 cal; Carbohydrates 4 g/15 cal; Fat 14 g/127 cal; (Saturated Fat 1 g/9 cal); Cholesterol 0 mg; Sodium 8 mg; Fiber 2 g; Vitamin A 19% of Daily Value

SAFFRON FETTUCINE
Calories 171; Protein 7 g/27 cal; Carbohydrates 30 g/118 cal; Fat 3 g/25 cal; (Saturated Fat .7 g/6 cal); Cholesterol 80 mg; Sodium 157 mg; Fiber 0 g; Iron 14% of Daily Value

SAUTEED SOFT SHELL CRABS
Calories 208; Protein 31 g/123 cal; Carbohydrates 1 g/4 cal; Fat 9 g/81 cal; (Saturated Fat .6 g/5 cal); Cholesterol 75 mg; Sodium 449 mg; Fiber 0 g; Calcium 29% of Daily Value

BLACKBERRY COBBLER

Cobblers are easy desserts to make. You can serve them with light whipped cream, ice cream, yogurt, frozen yogurt, or sorbet. You can also make delicious cobblers by mixing fruits and berries such as strawberry–rhubarb, peach–blackberry, peach–plum, or mango–raspberry.

Reserve the egg whites to make light whipped cream. Egg whites freeze well but need to be used as soon as they are defrosted.

Berry Mixture
4 cups (2 pints) blackberries
1 tablespoon Grand Marnier
1/2 cup sugar
1 tablespoon arrowroot
2 pinches cardamom

Biscuit Topping
1 cup unbleached flour

5 tablespoons sugar
1 teaspoon baking powder
1/2 teaspoon baking soda
1/2 teaspoon sea salt
3 tablespoons unsalted butter, cut into a 1/4-inch dice
1 egg yolk
1/3 cup buttermilk or 1/3 cup milk made sour with 1 tablespoon lemon juice

Preheat the oven to 400° F.

Combine the blackberries, Grand Marnier, sugar, arrowroot, and cardamom in a bowl. Butter an ovenproof 4 – 6 cup baking dish or ceramic pie plate and pour the berry mixture into the dish.

Sift and combine the flour, sugar, baking powder, baking soda, and salt in a medium bowl. Add the butter and work the dough quickly between your finger tips, until it is crumbly with a consistency like cornmeal. Or use a food processor, pulsing on and off, to mix. Add the egg yolk and buttermilk or soured milk, and stir to combine. The dough will be soft.

Spoon the dough onto the berries with a large serving spoon. Bake for 30 – 40 minutes, until the topping is browned and cooked through.

ASSEMBLY: Scoop a portion of cobbler on each of 4 luncheon plates. The berries should be quite liquid. Garnish with mint.

BLACKBERRY COBBLER
Calories 299;   Protein 5 g/18 cal;   Carbohydrates 51 g/203 cal;
Fat 9 g/78 cal;   (Saturated Fat 4 g/34 cal);   Cholesterol 57 mg;
Sodium 340 mg;   Fiber 6 g;   Vitamin C 40% of Daily Value

SPRING/SUMMER MENU VI

Restaurant Nora's Summer Vegetarian Plate:

BLACK BEANS, WHEATBERRIES, GRILLED TOMATOES, BUTTERNUT SQUASH PURÉE, SUGAR SNAPS, YELLOW BEANS, SNOW PEAS, CHARD, BROCCOLI RAPE, RED CHARD, AND CORN ON THE COB

WINE SELECTIONS

This full menu needs to be matched with either a red Merlot or a white Chardonnay.
Both wines will give a nice balance to so many different textures and flavors.

DeLoach Chardonnay 1990 Russian River

St Francis Merlot 1989 Sonoma Valley

Black Beans, Wheatberries, Grilled Tomatoes, Butternut Squash Purée, Sugar Snaps, Yellow Beans, Snow Peas, Chard, Broccoli Rape, Red Chard, and Corn On The Cob

BLACK BEANS

1½ cups black beans, soaked overnight, if possible

1 tablespoon olive oil

1 large onion, chopped

2 tablespoons chopped garlic

Peel from 1 orange

Juice from 1 orange

2 ancho chilies, seeded and torn into pieces (available in specialty stores)

2 chipotle chilies, seeded and torn into pieces (available in specialty stores)

1 large tomato, chopped, or 1 cup tomato juice

1 teaspoon cumin seed, preferably toasted

¼ cup chopped cilantro

Sea salt and freshly ground pepper

Pick through the beans to eliminate little stones or dirt, and rinse them briefly.

If you didn't soak the beans overnight, put them into a medium saucepan and add enough water to cover by 1 inch.

Bring to a boil, reduce the heat and simmer for 2 minutes. Remove the beans from the heat, cover and let rest 1 hour. Drain. This step is not necessary if you soak the beans overnight before cooking them.

Heat the olive oil in a sauté pan large enough to accommodate the beans, add the onion and garlic and sauté until softened, about 2 minutes. Add the drained beans and enough water to cover them by 2 inches.

Add the orange peel and juice, the ancho and chipotle chilies, the tomato or tomato juice, and cumin. Bring to a boil, reduce the heat, cover, and simmer for 1½ hours or until the beans are tender, the liquid absorbed, and the chilies disintegrated.

Add the cilantro and season to taste with salt and pepper. Remember that beans need a lot of salt.

Black beans are my favorite and Peter Seckman, who was the chef at Nora's years ago, perfected this method of preparing them. Peter was a southerner and a real bean specialist. Each time I go to Europe, I take black beans, a variety of dried chilies, and wild rice. These are considered exotic by my European friends.

Anchos are dried poblano chilies and they vary in hotness. If you grind them you get the chili powder used to make the famous Southwestern and Tex-Mex chilies. Chipotles are dried and smoked jalapeño chilies. They are always hot and add a great smoky flavor to any dish. Chipotle tomato sauce is one of my favorites and perfect for Southwestern or Mexican foods.

1 ½ cups wheatberries, soaked overnight, if possible
1 tablespoon chopped garlic
1 large onion, chopped
2 bay leaves
2 teaspoons thyme
2 ribs celery, chopped

1 small carrot, chopped
Grated peel of one lemon
1 tablespoon lemon juice
1 tablespoon olive oil
1 — 2 tablespoons chopped flat leaf parsley
1 teaspoon sea salt
Freshly ground black pepper

Put the wheatberries in a medium saucepan. Add water to cover by 2 inches. Bring to a boil and boil for 2 minutes. Take the saucepan off the heat, cover, and let it sit for 1 hour. This step can be omitted if you soak the wheatberries overnight.

Remove the lid and add enough water to cover the wheatberries by 1 inch. Stir in the garlic, onion, bay leaves, thyme, celery, carrot, and lemon peel. Cover, and simmer for 45 — 60 minutes, or until the berries are slightly puffed and softened.

Add the lemon juice, olive oil, parsley, and salt and pepper to taste, and stir to combine.

NORA'S VEGETARIAN PLATE

2 cups black beans,
2 cups wheatberries
4 grilled tomato halves (page 84)
1 ½ cups butternut squash purée (page 166)
4 ounces sugar snap peas (page 144)

4 ounces green beans (page 40)
4 ounces snow peas (page 127)
4 ounces Swiss red chard (page 40)
4 ounces broccoli rape (page 158)
2 ears corn on the cob, cut in half (page 84)

ASSEMBLY: Mound each vegetable on each of 4 large, warmed dinner plates, arranging them according to color and texture.

WHEATBERRIES PER SERVING
Calories 269;   Protein 8 g/31 cal;   Carbohydrates 50 g/200 cal;
Fat 4 g/38 cal;   (Saturated Fat .7 g/6 cal);   Cholesterol 0 mg;
Sodium 600 mg;   Fiber 14 g;   Vitamin A 51% of Daily Value

BLACK BEANS
Calories 184;   Protein 8 g/33 cal;   Carbohydrates 29 g/114 cal;
Fat 4 g/37 cal;   (Saturated Fat .6 g/5 cal);   Cholesterol 0 mg;
Sodium 15 mg;   Fiber 5 g;   Vitamin C 168% of Daily Value

SPRING/SUMMER VEGETARIAN MENU SUGGESTIONS

WATERMELON GAZPACHO (PAGE 95)
ARUGULA, RED AND YELLOW CHERRY TOMATOES, BLACK OLIVES AND FETA CHEESE (PAGE 82)
STIR-FRIED SUMMER VEGETABLES WITH TOFU AND TAMARI-GINGER DRESSING
BLACKBERRY COBBLER WITH LIGHT WHIPPED CREAM (PAGE 100)

GRILLED SUMMER VEGETABLES WITH HUMMUS (PAGE 97) OR
EGYPTIAN EGGPLANT-ROASTED RED PEPPER SALAD (PAGE 92) OR
GRILLED EGGPLANT WITH GOAT CHEESE AND ROASTED RED PEPPER-CORN RELISH (PAGE 88)
BABY LETTUCES WITH MELONS AND LIME DRESSING (PAGE 68)
SAFFRON FETTUCCINE WITH TOMATO-GREEN ONION SALAD (PAGE 99)
STRAWBERRIES WITH WARM CHOCOLATE SAUCE (PAGE 24)

JEWELL YAM VICHYSSOISE WITH CHIVE FLOWERS (PAGE 87)
TEN KINDS OF TOMATO SALAD WITH BASIL (PAGE 74)
WILD MUSHROOM AND LEEK TART WITH GOAT CHEESE AND WATERCRESS (PAGE 198)
RUSSIAN BLUEBERRY AND RASPBERRY PUDDING (PAGE 85) OR
VANILLA ICE CREAM WITH WARM PEACH-STRAWBERRY COMPOTE (PAGE 60)

ASPARAGUS AND MOREL MUSHROOMS WITH LEMON DRESSING (PAGE 55)
BABY LETTUCES WITH EDIBLE FLOWERS AND RASPBERRY VINAIGRETTE (PAGE 50)
SPAGHETTINI WITH TOMATO-GINGER SAUCE AND BROCCOLI (PAGE 125) OR
PASTA WITH EGYPTIAN EGGPLANT-ROASTED RED PEPPER SALAD (PAGE 92)
STRAWBERRY SHORTCAKE WITH LIGHT WHIPPED CREAM (PAGE 52) OR
PEACH PIE WITH VANILLA ICE CREAM (PAGE 44)

STEAMED ASPARAGUS WITH MUSTARD DRESSING OR ORANGE–GINGER DRESSING (PAGE 181)
ARUGULA AND TOMATO SALAD WITH EXTRA VIRGIN OLIVE OIL VINAIGRETTE (PAGE 82)
CREAMY POLENTA WITH SAUTÉED MOREL MUSHROOMS (PAGE 157)
PEACHES IN RED WINE WITH MINT (PAGE 93)

AUTUMN

AUTUMN MENU I

CORN CHOWDER WITH DILL

MANGO AND BRIE QUESADILLA WITH WATERCRESS AND TOMATO SALSA

ROASTED MUSCOVY DUCK BREAST WITH DRIED CRANBERRY-BALSAMIC SAUCE, PUMPKIN PURÉE, AND BRUSSELS SPROUTS

BIBB LETTUCE WITH PARSLEY-CHIVE DRESSING

WINE SELECTIONS

A soft, spicy Zinfandel from California would work well with the tangy cranberry-duck combination.

Frog's Leap 1990 Napa Valley

Ridge Lytton Springs 1989 Sonoma Valley

CORN CHOWDER WITH DILL

2 tablespoons butter
1 large onion, chopped
2 teaspoons minced garlic
1 carrot, small dice
2 stalks celery, small dice including the leaves
3 ears corn, about 2 cups kernels, cut from
    the cob

3 – 4 cups duck or chicken stock or 2 chicken
    bouillon cubes dissolved in 3 – 4 cups
    water
Sea salt and freshly ground black pepper
1 small red pepper, diced
2 tablespoons chopped dill for garnish

Melt the butter in a medium saucepan over low heat. Add the onion, garlic, carrot, and celery and sauté for 10 – 15 minutes, stirring frequently. Add the corn and 3 cups stock or bouillon. Season to taste with salt and pepper. Simmer for about 10 minutes. If the chowder is too thick, add the remaining stock or bouillon. Stir in the red pepper and 1 tablespoon of the dill.

ASSEMBLY: Pour the hot soup into 4 warmed soup bowls. Garnish with the remaining dill.

CORN CHOWDER WITH DILL
Calories 182;   Protein 4 g/15 cal;   Carbohydrates 27 g/107 cal;
Fat 7 g/60 cal;   (Saturated Fat 4 g/34 cal);   Cholesterol 16 mg;
Sodium 235 mg;   Fiber 4 g;   Vitamin A 47% of Daily Value

When you cut the kernels off the cob, do so over a plate to catch the sweet and starchy juices. Add these to the chowder. The sugar in corn turns to starch quickly, so the fresher the corn, the sweeter. In fact, home-grown or fresh farm stand corn is so sweet and tender you can eat it raw. I prefer yellow corn for its beautiful color.

I often add a pinch of saffron to the chowder to give it an even brighter color. If you prefer a thicker chowder, use a skimmer or slotted spoon to remove a cup of cooked vegetables, purée them in the blender, and return them to the soup. Chowder is a good way to use fresh corn when there is an abundance of it. I like to triple this recipe and freeze the extra for future meals.

Mango and Brie Quesadilla with Watercress and Tomato Salsa

This uncooked salsa is also known as "pico de gallo." Literally, "rooster's beak," this name refers to the way a rooster chops up his food.

Salsas are fast replacing traditional heavy cream and butter sauces. I like to make all sorts using fruits like grapefruit, orange, mango, papaya, and pineapple, or vegetables such as roasted red pepper, corn, and black beans.

You can crisp the tortillas by heating them briefly, one at a time, in a dry sauté pan or on a preheated grill. I often make these quesadillas with goat cheese and mozzarella instead of the Brie.

Quesadillas are a favorite meal on Sunday night when I am home with my family. I stuff them with leftover cooked chicken or duck, beans, spinach, and goat cheese. They make an interesting and easy supper when served with salad and fruit and nuts for dessert.

TOMATO SALSA

1 pound tomatoes, cut in half, seeds squeezed out
1 jalapeño chili, seeds removed and minced
1/4 teaspoon ground cumin
1/2 teaspoon minced garlic
1 tablespoon minced shallot or red onion
1/4 cup packed cilantro leaves, chopped
Juice of 1 lime
Sea salt and freshly ground black pepper

Cut the tomatoes into even, 1/4-inch cubes. Put them into a bowl with the chili, cumin, garlic, shallot, cilantro, and lime juice. Add salt and pepper to taste.

MANGO AND BRIE QUESADILLA

Eight 6-inch flour tortillas
2 mangoes (about 1 pound each), peeled and sliced
8 ounces Brie, sliced
Freshly ground black pepper
1 bunch watercress, washed, stems removed, and spun dry
Tomato salsa

Preheat oven to 400° F.

Lay 4 of the tortillas directly on a rack in the preheated oven and bake for 3 minutes or until crisp. This prevents the bottom of the quesadilla from getting soggy when filled and baked. Remove from the oven.

Place the crisped tortillas on a baking sheet and put some sliced mango on each. Divide the Brie among the tortillas, placing the cheese in the center so it will not run out the sides as it melts. Season to taste with black pepper. Cover with the remaining four tortillas.

Turn the oven down to 375° F and bake the quesadillas for 4 – 5 minutes, until the Brie starts to melt and the quesadillas are crisp.

ASSEMBLY: Put a quesadilla on each of 4 warmed, dinner plates and cut into fourths. Arrange a nest of watercress in the center of each quesadilla and spoon tomato salsa into the middle of each nest.

TOMATO SALSA
Calories 37;   Protein 2 g/6 cal;   Carbohydrates 7 g/28 cal;
Fat .3 g/3 cal;   (Saturated Fat 0 g/0 cal);   Cholesterol 0 mg;
Sodium 115 mg;   Fiber 2 g;   Vitamin C 72% of Daily Value

MANGO AND BRIE QUESADILLA
Calories 530;   Protein 22 g/87 cal;   Carbohydrates 67 g/268 cal;
Fat 19 g/175 cal;   (Saturated Fat 1 g/12 cal);   Cholesterol 56 mg;
Sodium 601 mg;   Fiber 3 g;   Calcium 31% of Daily Value

ROASTED MUSCOVY DUCK BREAST WITH DRIED CRANBERRY-BALSAMIC SAUCE, PUMPKIN PURÉE, AND BRUSSELS SPROUTS

PUMPKIN PURÉE ✳

2 pounds pumpkin or butternut squash
Sea salt and freshly ground black pepper

Pinch of raz el hanout or garam masala
(see page 174), or a pinch of ground nutmeg

Preheat oven to 375° F.

Cut the pumpkin or squash in half, scrape out the seeds, and place, cut-side-down, on a baking sheet. Bake for about 50 minutes or until pumpkin is soft.

Scoop the pulp into a blender or food processor. Season to taste with raz el hanout, garam masala, or nutmeg, and salt and pepper. Process until smooth.

You can also peel and chop the pumpkin or squash and steam it in a medium saucepan using a collapsible steamer. But I warn you—peeling raw pumpkin isn't easy.

To prepare your own raz el honout or garam masala see page 174.

BRUSSELS SPROUTS

½ pound Brussels sprouts

Remove the outer leaves from the Brussels sprouts and make a cross in the base to shorten the cooking time. Steam for 15 – 30 minutes, depending on their size, until the sprouts are bright green and cooked through.

I find I can coax my customers into eating unusual vegetables if I purée them. For example, even the unpopular beet finds new fans when I purée it with sautéed onions, boiled potatoes, caraway seeds, and salt and pepper.

DRIED CRANBERRY-BALSAMIC SAUCE ✳

½ cup dried cranberries
2 cups duck stock or chicken or veal stock or 1
  beef or chicken bouillon cube dissolved in
  2 cups water

2 tablespoons port wine or madeira
4 shallots, peeled
1½ tablespoons balsamic vinegar
Sea salt and freshly ground black pepper

Preheat the oven to 400° F.

Put the shallots in a small, non-reactive baking dish. Dress with 1 teaspoon olive oil and season with salt and pepper. Cover with aluminum foil and roast for 30 – 40 minutes, until soft.

Put the cranberries in a medium saucepan, add 1½ cups of stock and wine, and simmer for 5 minutes or until the cranberries are plumped. Remove ¼ cup of the plumped cranberries with a slotted spoon and reserve for garnish.

Put the remaining cranberries in a blender with the shallots and vinegar, and purée until smooth. Add the remaining stock, if necessary, to thin the purée until it has a sauce-like consistency. Season to taste with salt and pepper.

Dried cranberries are sweetened with fruit juices so are much sweeter than fresh cranberries. If you can't find dried cranberries, substitute tart or sweet dried cherries or even dried blueberries.

*You can bone the duck the day before you
roast it.*

*4 boneless duck breasts (½ pound each)
Sea salt and freshly ground black pepper*

*Pumpkin purée
Brussels sprouts
Dried cranberry-balsamic sauce
Reserved plumped cranberries for garnish*

Preheat the oven to 400° F.

Dry the duck breasts with paper towels and season to taste with salt and pepper. Heat a dry sauté pan and put the duck breast in the pan, skin-side-down, to render some of the fat from under the skin and to crisp the skin at the same time. Continue sautéing for about 10 minutes over medium heat. Turn the breasts over and put them in the oven for 10 – 15 minutes, until cooked to desired doneness—about 10 minutes for medium-rare, 15 minutes for medium.

Remove the breasts from the oven, put them on a platter, cover with foil to keep warm and allow them to cool for 2 – 3 minutes before slicing.

ASSEMBLY: Cut the duck breasts into thin slices. Use a very sharp, serrated knife because the skin will be crisp. Fan the slices into a semi-circle on the lower half of 4 warm dinner plates. Put a big spoonful of pumpkin purée in the top center of the semi-circle.

Arrange 3 Brussels sprouts on each side of the fanned breast. Pour the dried cranberry-balsamic sauce evenly over the sliced duck. Sprinkle each plate with some of the reserved plumped cranberries.

PUMPKIN PURÉE
Calories 106; Protein 2 g/8 cal; Carbohydrates 24 g/96 cal;
Fat .2 g/2 cal; (Saturated Fat 0 g/0 cal); Cholesterol 0 mg;
Sodium 9 mg; Fiber 4 g; Calcium 11% of Daily Value

BRUSSELS SPROUTS
Calories 30; Protein 2 g/8 cal; Carbohydrates 5 g/20 cal;
Fat .1 g/1 cal; (Saturated Fat 0 g/0 cal); Cholesterol 0 mg;
Sodium 14 mg; Fiber 2 g; Vitamin C 80% of Daily Value

DRIED CRANBERRY-BALSAMIC SAUCE
Calories 291; Protein 61 g/245 cal; Carbohydrates 9 g/35 cal;
Fat 1 g/11 cal; (Saturated Fat .6 g/5 cal); Cholesterol 3 mg;
Sodium 557 mg; Fiber 1 g; Vitamin A 15% of Daily Value

ROASTED MUSCOVY DUCK BREAST
Calories 227; Protein 48 g/190 cal; Carbohydrates 0 g/0 cal;
Fat 10 g/87 cal; (Saturated Fat 3 g/27 cal); Cholesterol 63 mg;
Sodium 128 mg; Fiber 0 g; Iron 68% of Daily Value

BIBB LETTUCE WITH PARSLEY-CHIVE DRESSING

1 cup flat leaf parsley leaves, tightly packed
1 bunch chives, trimmed and chopped
½ teaspoon minced garlic
2 tablespoons white wine vinegar
Peel of ½ lemon
3 tablespoons water
¼ cup olive oil

Sea salt and freshly ground black pepper

4 small heads Bibb lettuce, washed, trimmed,
    and patted dry
½ medium red bell pepper, cut into ¼-inch
    cubes for garnish

I like puréed, emulsified herb dressings. I find the flavor of the herbs much stronger when puréed.

You can even make edible flower vinaigrette using flowers that are slightly past their prime and reserving the best petals to garnish the finished salad. Make certain that the flowers are pesticide-free though. Try using roses, marigold petals, or any herb flower, like chive or thyme.

Make the dressing by adding the parsley, ½ of the chives, garlic, vinegar, lemon peel, water, and olive oil to a blender. Purée until smooth. Season to taste with salt and pepper.

Cut each head of Bibb lettuce into 4 wedges.

ASSEMBLY: Arrange each quartered head of Bibb lettuce in a windmill pattern on each of 4 dinner plates. Pour some of the parsley dressing into the center of these wedges. Garnish with pepper cubes and the remaining chives.

PARSLEY-CHIVE DRESSING
Calories 119;   Protein 1 g/3 cal;   Carbohydrates 4 g/17 cal;
Fat 11 g/99 cal;   (Saturated Fat 2 g/14 cal);   Cholesterol 0 mg;
Sodium 9 mg;   Fiber 1 g;   Vitamin C 40% of Daily Value

BIBB WEDGES
Calories 32;   Protein 2 g/9 cal;   Carbohydrates 5 g/21 cal;
Fat .2 g/2 cal;   (Saturated Fat .1 g/1 cal);   Cholesterol 0 mg;
Sodium 10 mg;   Fiber 2 g;   Vitamin C 67% of Daily Value

AUTUMN MENU II

CHANTERELLE MUSHROOM, SPINACH, AND HAM BRUSCHETTA

BAKED HALIBUT WITH THREE COLORED PEPPERS AND RED BLISS AND FINGERLING POTATOES

TOMATO SALAD WITH GOAT CHEESE AND EXTRA-VIRGIN OLIVE OIL DRESSING

PEARS POACHED IN SAUTERNES WITH WARM CHOCOLATE SAUCE AND LIGHT WHIPPED CREAM

WINE SELECTIONS

*An austere Chablis will well match this very subtle halibut. White wine and fish
is a good combination, but Chablis and fish is even better.*

Chablis Montmain 1986 Gerard Duplessis

Chablis Valmur 1986 J. Moreau

CHANTERELLE MUSHROOM, SPINACH, AND HAM BRUSCHETTA

Four ³/₄-inch thick slices Italian country bread
1 clove garlic, peeled
4 teaspoons olive oil
3 tablespoons minced shallots
1 teaspoon minced garlic
½ pound chanterelle mushrooms, wiped clean
*   or briefly washed, drained, dried, with*
*   large ones thickly sliced*

1 teaspoon dry sherry wine or balsamic vinegar
2 ounces spinach or arugula, stemmed and cut
*   in julienne*
4 ounces smoked ham or tongue, cut in julienne
Sea salt and freshly ground pepper
2 tablespoons chopped parsley for garnish

Make the bruschetta by toasting or grilling the bread until crusty and firm. Rub the bread slices generously on one side with the garlic.

Heat the olive oil in a medium sauté pan, add the minced shallots and the garlic, and sauté for about 3 minutes. Add the chanterelles and cook on a medium-high heat for about 5 minutes, until the mushrooms are wilted. Add the sherry or balsamic vinegar and cook over high heat for about 1 minute to reduce. Add the spinach or arugula and the ham or tongue and sauté, stirring until the greens are slightly wilted and the meat is warmed, 1 – 2 minutes. Taste for seasoning and be careful with the salt—cured meat is often very salty.

ASSEMBLY: Put each bruschetta on a warmed dinner plate and spoon the chanterelle mixture on top. Garnish with parsley and the juices from the sauté pan or with some of the vinaigrette from the tomato salad.

CHANTERELLE MUSHROOM, SPINACH, AND HAM BRUSCHETTA
Calories 193;   Protein 12 g/47 cal;   Carbohydrates 23 g/93 cal;
Fat 6 g/53 cal;   (Saturated Fat 1 g/13 cal);   Cholesterol 16 mg;
Sodium 468 mg;   Fiber 2 g;   Vitamin C 31% of Daily Value

Bruschetta is the Italian word for toasted bread, which normally is brushed with olive oil and rubbed with garlic.

Because we buy whole organic animals at Nora's, Than, our Cambodian butcher, has become an expert at curing hams, bacon, and tongues and smoking them with applewood for added flavor. We have even begun curing our own prosciutto.

Baked Halibut with Three Colored Peppers and Red Bliss and Fingerling Potatoes

Halibut, a member of the flounder family, are abundant in the northern Atlantic and Pacific waters and generally weigh between 50 and 100 pounds. I was amused to learn that Atlantic halibut are right-eyed and Pacific halibut are left-eyed.

I often enrich this dish by adding a dollop of aioli (recipe, page 66) to each fillet.

I introduced Ward and Cass of Flickerville Farm to fingerlings and brought them seed potatoes because I remembered how delicious they tasted. My mother bought them every fall from a peddler who went door to door with a pushcart. I am happy that I can now buy so many varieties of potatoes, not just the Idaho and Maine varieties which were the only ones available when I first came to the USA.

Among the potatoes we serve at Nora's are Yellow Finn, Russian Banana Fingerlings, Red Bliss, Yukon Gold, and all kinds of purple potatoes.

Baked Halibut with Three Colored Peppers

4 teaspoons olive oil
1 medium onion, thinly sliced
2 teaspoons minced garlic
2 green peppers, seeded and cut in julienne
1 red pepper, seeded and cut in julienne
1 yellow pepper, seeded and cut in julienne
1 cup white wine

2 to 3 tablespoons assorted herbs such as thyme, oregano, and rosemary
Sea salt and freshly ground black pepper
1 1/2 pounds halibut fillets, cut into 4 portions
Small bouquet of assorted herbs such as thyme, oregano, and rosemary, for garnish

Preheat the oven to 450° F.

Heat 2 teaspoons of the olive oil in a medium sauté pan, add the onion, garlic, and peppers and sauté for about 5 minutes, stirring frequently. Add the wine and herbs and season to taste with salt and pepper. Bring the mixture to a boil, and cook for about 1 minute, stirring to combine. Remove the pan from the heat.

Spoon the pepper mixture and juices into a baking dish large enough to accommodate the fillets in one layer. Arrange the halibut fillets on top. Drizzle with the remaining olive oil and season to taste with salt and pepper. Bake for 8 – 10 minutes, until the fish is cooked through.

Red Bliss and Fingerling Potatoes

16 to 20 small red bliss and/or
    fingerling potatoes, about 1 pound, unpeeled

Steam the potatoes in a medium saucepan using a collapsible insert or boil them for 10 to 15 minutes, until a fork can be easily inserted in the potato.

Assembly: Use a spatula to transfer each halibut fillet with the pepper mixture and juices under it to the center of a large warm dinner plate. Surround the fish with the potatoes and garnish with a small bouquet of fresh herbs.

BAKED HALIBUT
Calories 294;   Protein 37 g/149 cal;   Carbohydrates 16 g/63 cal;
Fat 9 g/82 cal;   (Saturated Fat 1 g/11 cal);   Cholesterol 54 mg;
Sodium 102 mg;   Fiber 3 g;   Iron 29% of Daily Value

RED BLISS AND FINGRERLING POTATOES
Calories 69;   Protein 3 g/12 cal;   Carbohydrates 14 g/56 cal;
Fat .1 g/1 cal;   (Saturated Fat 0 g/0 cal);   Cholesterol 0 mg;
Sodium 11 mg;   Fiber 4 g;   Iron 24% of Daily Value

TOMATO SALAD WITH GOAT CHEESE AND EXTRA-VIRGIN OLIVE OIL DRESSING*

This is a simple salad where the ingredients speak for themselves: mild white goat cheese, ripe red tomatoes, and fragrant green basil all dressed with flavorful extra-virgin olive oil.

A 55 gallon drum of extra-virgin olive oil is dropped off in front of Nora's once a month. It comes from an Italian family and is wonderful.

1 teaspoon lemon juice
Sea salt and freshly ground black pepper
2 tablespoons extra-virgin olive oil

2 large beefsteak tomatoes or 4 medium tomatoes, sliced (1¼ pounds)

2 ounces log-shaped goat cheese, sliced into 4 rounds
Basil leaves for garnish

Make the dressing by pouring the lemon juice into a small bowl, and dissolving the salt and pepper in it. Beat in the olive oil with a fork or a small whisk.

ASSEMBLY: Place the tomato slices in a circle on 4 dinner plates and put the goat cheese in the center. Spoon some dressing on the tomatoes. Garnish with basil leaves.

TOMATO SALAD WITH GOAT CHEESE
Calories 58;   Protein 3 g/10 cal;   Carbohydrates 6 g/22 cal;
Fat 3 g/26 cal;   (Saturated Fat 2 g/20 cal);   Cholesterol 13 mg;
Sodium 56 mg;   Fiber 1 g;   Vitamin C 36% of Daily Value

EXTRA-VIRGIN OLIVE OIL DRESSING
Calories 62;   Protein 0 g/0 cal;   Carbohydrates .25 g/1 cal;
Fat 7 g/61 cal;   (Saturated Fat 1 g/9 cal);   Cholesterol 0 mg;
Sodium 0 mg;   Fiber 0 g;   Vitamin C 1% of Daily Value

Pears Poached in Sauternes with Warm Chocolate Sauce and Light Whipped Cream

4 Bosc or Anjou pears, peeled
½ bottle or 2 cups Sauternes or sweet
   dessert wine
Peel from ½ lemon
4 whole cloves

2 ounces of semisweet chocolate
¼ cup light whipped cream (page 53),
   for garnish
Fresh mint leaves for garnish

Remove the core and seeds from the pears, leaving them whole. Use a small melon baller or pointed vegetable peeler and start from the bottom of the pears.

Pour the Sauternes into a small non-reactive saucepan just large enough to hold the pears. Add the lemon peel and the cloves and bring to a boil. Add the pears, reduce the heat, cover the pot and simmer until tender, 10 – 15 minutes. Turn the pears from time to time so that they cook evenly.

Remove the pears from the saucepan. If you have more than ½ cup liquid, boil the wine a little longer, until reduced to a ½ cup with the consistency of syrup. Remove the saucepan from the heat, add the chocolate and stir to melt and combine. The sauce will thicken as it cools.

ASSEMBLY: Place each pear in a deep dessert plate and spoon some of the cooled chocolate sauce over and around it. Garnish with a dollop of light whipped cream and a mint leaf.

PEARS POACHED IN SAUTERNES
Calories 157; Protein 1 g/5 cal; Carbohydrates 35 g/141 cal;
Fat 1 g/11 cal; (Saturated Fat 0 g/0 cal); Cholesterol 0 mg;
Sodium 13 mg; Fiber 6 g; Vitamin C 16% of Daily Value

CHOCOLATE SAUCE
Calories 91; Protein 2 g/6 cal; Carbohydrates 5 g/18 cal;
Fat 7 g/67 cal; (Saturated Fat 3 g/27 cal); Cholesterol 0 mg;
Sodium 0 mg; Fiber 1 g; Iron 6% of Daily Value

These pears are cooked in a small amount of liquid and turned to cook evenly so that you don't need to use much wine but the poaching liquid is intense and flavorful with little reduction.

Sauternes, made from Semillon, Sauvignon, and Muscatele grapes shriveled to concentrated ripeness by the botrytis fungus or "noble rot," is the most prized and most expensive of Bordeaux's sweet white wines. Barsac, an almost equally admired sweet wine from Bordeaux, can be used instead of Sauternes. Other dessert wines which work well are Late Harvest wines from California and German Beerenauslese.

AUTUMN MENU III

PUMPKIN SOUP WITH PEPITAS

CARPACCIO WITH ARUGULA, PARMESAN, AND MUSTARD-CAPER DRESSING

CRAB AND SHIITAKE CAKES WITH TOMATO-GINGER SAUCE, SAUTÉED TAT SOI, AND SNOW PEAS

APPLE-WALNUT-RAISIN STRUDEL WITH LIGHT WHIPPED CREAM

WINE SELECTIONS

Beer and Crab cakes are a nice combination. Pinot Noir, a red wine, also complements crabs.
A medium to full-bodied wine is necessary for all the different flavors in this menu.

Ponzi 1990 Willamette Valley, Oregon

Blagny 1990 Joseph Matrot

Pumpkin Soup with Pepitas*

2 — 2 1/2 pounds pumpkin
2 teaspoons canola oil
1 onion, chopped
1 celery rib, chopped
2 cups milk
2 cups water
2 tablespoons lemon juice

1/4 teaspoon cumin
Pinch allspice
2 tablespoons dry sherry or marsala
Sea salt and freshly ground black pepper
2 tablespoons pepitas or pumpkin seeds
     for garnish

Pepitas are green pumpkin seeds and a popular ingredient in Mexican cooking. Pepitas can be bought in specialty stores and are available salted, roasted, or raw.

Fall and the holidays mean pumpkin at Nora's. During these months we serve pumpkin in all forms: pie, muffins, risotto, custard and purée. With this abundance of pumpkin, I aim to satisfy my customers' appetite for it so that they won't miss pumpkin until it comes into season again. I believe in this way of eating: feast on what is seasonal and abundant, and when the season returns the next year you'll be ready for those tastes again.

Preheat the oven to 350° F.

Cut the pumpkin in half, scrape out the seeds, and place it, cut-side-down, on a baking sheet or baking dish. Bake about 40 minutes, until tender and easily pierced with a fork. Allow the pumpkin to cool for 10 minutes before proceeding, as it will be easier to handle when not so hot.

While the pumpkin is baking, heat the oil in a small sauté pan and sauté the onion and celery for about 3 minutes, until softened and clear.

Scoop out the pumpkin pulp with a large spoon, put it into a large bowl, and add the onion, celery, milk, and water. Stir to combine. Ladle some of this mixture into a blender and purée it in batches, being careful not to overfill the blender. Strain the soup through a colander to remove remaining fiber or seeds. Add the lemon juice, cumin, allspice, and sherry. Season to taste with salt and pepper.

Spread the pepitas or pumpkin seeds on a baking sheet and roast in the oven for 10 minutes or until toasted.

ASSEMBLY: Reheat the soup, divide it among 4 warmed soup bowls and sprinkle with the pepitas or pumpkin seeds.

PUMPKIN SOUP
Calories 192;   Protein 8 g/31 cal;   Carbohydrates 32 g/126 cal;
Fat 4 g/35 cal;   (Saturated Fat 1 g/10 cal);   Cholesterol 5 mg;
Sodium 96 mg;   Fiber 6 g;   Vitamin A 66% of Daily Value

CARPACCIO WITH ARUGULA, PARMESAN AND MUSTARD-CAPER SAUCE*

Carpaccio is a great favorite at Nora's, and our customers especially like our lean and flavorful organic beef.

Two of my popular variations on this traditional Italian first-course are: Southwestern carpaccio served with an ancho chili dressing, homemade tortillas, thin curls of Monterey Jack cheese, and a sprinkle of black beans; and Chinese carpaccio served with a ginger-tamari vinaigrette, mizuna, grilled shiitakes, and garnished with a sprinkle of crispy noodles.

1 tablespoon mustard
1 tablespoon small capers
1 teaspoon balsamic vinegar
1 tablespoon olive oil
Freshly ground black pepper

½ pound eye of the round, partially frozen to facilitate slicing
2 ounces Parmesan
4 ounces arugula, washed, spun dry, and cut in julienne

Make the mustard-caper sauce by putting the mustard, capers, and vinegar into a small bowl. Add the oil while whisking with a fork to emulsify the sauce. Season to taste with pepper.

Cut the eye of the round into as thin slices as possible with the sharpest slicing knife you own. You might ask your butcher to slice the meat for you with an electric meat slicer into ¹⁄₁₆-inch slices.

ASSEMBLY: Spread a thin layer of the mustard sauce on the center of 4 salad plates. Cover with overlapping slices of beef. Use a vegetable peeler to shave thin curls of Parmesan onto the plates. Garnish with arugula. Serve cold.

MUSTARD CAPER SAUCE
Calories 36; Protein .25 g/1 cal; Carbohydrates 1 g/3 cal;
Fat 4 g/32 cal; (Saturated Fat .4 g/4 cal); Cholesterol 0 mg;
Sodium 135 mg; Fiber 0 g

CARPACCIO WITH ARUGULA AND PARMESAN
Calories 183; Protein 17 g/68 cal; Carbohydrates 2 g/6 cal;
Fat 12 g/109 cal; (Saturated Fat 3 g/30 cal); Cholesterol 44 mg;
Sodium 277 mg; Fiber 1 g; Iron 11% of Daily Value

CRAB AND SHIITAKE CAKES WITH TOMATO-GINGER SAUCE, SAUTEED TAT SOI, AND SNOW PEAS

TOMATO-GINGER SAUCE ✳

1 tablespoon canola oil
2 tablespoons chopped shallots
1 tablespoon minced garlic
1¹/₂ pounds tomatoes, coarsely chopped

2-inch piece of ginger, peeled and sliced thinly
  across the fibers
Sea salt and freshly ground black pepper

Ginger and tomatoes are a great flavor combination. Use this sauce with Asian noodles or pasta, adding tat soi, carrots, bok choy, and shrimp or chicken to make a wonderful simple meal.

Heat the oil in a medium saucepan, add the shallots and garlic, and sauté until soft, stirring from time to time. Add the tomatoes and ginger, stir, and bring to a boil. Reduce the heat and simmer about 5 minutes. Remove from the heat. Cool slightly and purée in a blender until smooth. Season to taste with salt and pepper.

The crabmeat you buy has been cooked in the process of removing it from the shell, so you want to heat the crab cake just enough to cook the eggs. I often omit the eggs altogether and substitute 2 – 4 tablespoons of parsnip, carrot, or sunchoke purée to bind the crabcakes.

4 tablespoons canola oil
2 tablespoons shallots, minced
1 tablespoon garlic, minced
3 ribs celery, washed and minced
1 small carrot, minced
1 small red or yellow pepper, seeded and minced
½ pound shiitakes, washed, stemmed, and sliced

2 eggs, beaten or 4 egg whites, beaten
4 tablespoons minced cilantro
1 pound jumbo lump crabmeat, picked through to remove shell particles
Sea salt and freshly ground black pepper
4 tablespoons finely ground breadcrumbs (optional)

Heat the oil in a medium sauté pan. Add the shallots and garlic and sauté, stirring, for about 1 minute. Add the celery and carrot, lower the heat, and cook until softened, about 2 minutes. Add the peppers and the shiitakes, stir, and sauté until the mushrooms are soft and cooked through, about 3 minutes. Remove from the heat and allow to cool for 10 minutes.

Preheat the broiler.

Combine the sautéed vegetables with the eggs, cilantro, and crabmeat, being careful not to break up the lumps of crab. Season to taste with salt and pepper.

Make 12 small crab cakes. They will be very soft and delicate. Cover the outside with breadcrumbs (optional). Put the crab cakes on a sheet pan. Broil them, on one side only, for 3 – 4 minutes, until nicely browned. Do not turn. They are too delicate.

2 teaspoons canola oil
¼ pound snow peas

¼ pound tat soi
Sea salt and freshly ground pepper

Tat soi is a Chinese green that grows in small, loose rosettes. Ward Sinclair at Flickerville Farm introduced it to me about two years ago. It's like a crunchy, sharp spinach.

Heat the oil in a medium sauté pan. Add the snow peas and sauté for 2 minutes. Add the tat soi and sauté for another 2 minutes, until the vegetables are bright green and slightly softened. Season to taste with salt and pepper.

ASSEMBLY: Pour a pool of the tomato-ginger sauce in the center of 4 warm dinner plates. Arrange 3 crab cakes on each plate. Place 2 or 3 snow peas between each crab cake and pile the tat soi in the center.

CRAB AND SHIITAKE CAKES
Calories 304; Protein 26 g/102 cal; Carbohydrates 14 g/55 cal; Fat 16 g/147 cal; (Saturated Fat 3 g/27 cal); Cholesterol 1 mg; Sodium 446 mg; Fiber 3 g; Calcium 21% of Daily Value

TAT SOI AND SNOW PEAS
Calories 41; Protein 2 g/7 cal; Carbohydrates 3 g/12 cal; Fat 2 g/22 cal; (Saturated Fat .2 g/2 cal); Cholesterol 0 mg; Sodium 23 mg; Fiber 2 g; Vitamin A 24% of Daily Value

TOMATO-GINGER SAUCE
Calories 87; Protein 2 g/8 cal; Carbohydrates 11 g/43 cal; Fat 4 g/36 cal; (Saturated Fat .3 g/3 cal); Cholesterol 0 mg; Sodium 17 mg; Fiber 2 g; Vitamin C 57% of Daily Value

Apple-Walnut-Raisin Strudel with Light Whipped Cream

4 sheets defrosted Greek filo or strudel dough, available at specialty stores
2 tablespoons melted unsalted butter
1 tablespoon fine bread crumbs
1 tablespoon sugar
1 pound tart apples such as Granny Smith, quartered, cored, and thinly sliced

¼ cup raisins, plumped in hot water for 2 minutes
¼ cup walnuts, coarsely chopped
Powdered sugar, for garnish
Light whipped cream (page 53)
Fresh mint for garnish

My mother always kept strudel leaves in the refrigerator when I was growing up. They are actually thicker than filo leaves so you would use only two sheets instead of four to make this apple strudel, which is a traditional Viennese dessert.

Preheat the oven to 375° F.

Moisten a kitchen towel under cold running water and wring it out until nearly dry. Spread the towel out on a work surface.

Take out the first sheet of filo and lay it on the towel. Cover the remaining filo with another towel so it will not dry out while you work. Use a pastry brush to spread the filo with some of the melted butter. Sprinkle with some of the bread crumbs and some of the sugar. Put the next filo sheet on top and repeat the procedure. Continue with the third and fourth sheets.

Spread out the apples on top of the prepared filo sheets leaving a 3-inch border on the long side away from you and narrow borders around the other sides. Sprinkle with the raisins and walnuts and any leftover bread crumbs and sugar.

Pick up the towel edge closest to you and use it to shape the strudel into a jelly roll, lifting and rolling it away from you toward the back edge of the dough. Use the towel to pick up and transfer the strudel to a baking sheet. Roll it off the towel onto the baking sheet. Tuck the ends under and brush with the remaining butter.

Score the top layer of filo dough into 4 portions using a sharp knife. This prevents the strudel from flaking too much when you cut it after it comes out of the oven.

Bake the strudel for about 40 minutes, until the apples are cooked and juicy and the strudel is golden brown.

Assembly: Cut the strudel into 4 servings along the scored lines and arrange each one on a dinner plate. Dust with powdered sugar. Add a dollop of light whipped cream and garnish with mint.

APPLE-WALNUT RAISIN STRUDEL
Calories 320;   Protein 5 g/21 cal;   Carbohydrates 48 g/193 cal;
Fat 12 g/106 cal;   (Saturated Fat 4 g/39 cal);   Cholesterol 17 mg;
Sodium 176 mg;   Fiber 3 g;   Iron 10% of Daily Value

AUTUMN MENU IV

SMOKED TROUT WITH HORSERADISH SAUCE AND APPLES

MESCLUN LETTUCES WITH LEMON DRESSING

INDONESIAN QUAIL SATÉ WITH LEMON BASMATI RICE, MUSTARD GREENS, TOMATO SALAD, PEANUT SAUCE, AND CHILI-CUCUMBER RELISH

CHOCOLATE SORBET WITH RASPBERRIES

WINE SELECTIONS

The Indonesian spices need a firm wine to accompany them.
A red St. Julian or a Cabernet Sauvignon is the right strength for this delicious quail menu.

Chateau Beycheville 1985, France

Spottswoode 1988 Napa Valley, California

SMOKED TROUT WITH HORSERADISH SAUCE AND APPLES*

4 tablespoons grated fresh horseradish or 2
    tablespoons drained prepared horseradish
1/4 cup low-fat yogurt drained for at least 1/2
    an hour, or 1/4 cup sour cream
1 tablespoon lemon juice

Sea salt and freshly ground black pepper
1 apple, sliced into thin wedges
1 bunch fresh dill for garnish

2 whole smoked trout (10 ounces each)

Skin, bone, and divide the trout into 4 fillets.

Mix the horseradish with the yogurt or sour cream. Add the lemon juice and season to taste with salt and pepper.

ASSEMBLY: Place a trout fillet on each of 4 dinner plates, arrange a spoonful of horseradish sauce next to it and fan the apple slices out on the side. Garnish generously with sprigs of dill.

APPLES AND HORSERADISH SAUCE
Calories 60;   Protein 2 g/8 cal;   Carbohydrates 13 g/50 cal;
Fat .2 g/2 cal;   (Saturated Fat 0 g/0 cal);   Cholesterol 0 mg;
Sodium 15 mg;   Fiber 1 g;   Calcium 11% of Daily Value

SMOKED TROUT (5 OUNCES)
Calories 70;   Protein 10 g/40 cal;   Carbohydrates 0 g/0 cal;
Fat 2 g/20 cal;   (Saturated Fat 1 g/10 cal);   Cholesterol 40 mg;
Sodium 540 mg;   Fiber 0 g;   Iron 4% of Daily Value

MESCLUN LETTUCES WITH LEMON DRESSING*

1 tablespoon lemon juice
1 teaspoon of grated lemon peel
2 tablespoons chopped chives
3 tablespoons extra-virgin olive oil

Sea salt and freshly ground black pepper

8 ounces mesclun lettuces, washed and spun dry

Mix the lemon juice, lemon peel, chives, and olive oil in a small bowl or a jar with a screw top lid. Add salt and pepper to taste. Mix with a fork or shake to combine.

ASSEMBLY: Toss the mesclun lettuces with the dressing and divide them among 4 dinner plates.

LEMON DRESSING
Calories 96;   Protein .25 g/1 cal;   Carbohydrates 1 g/3 cal;
Fat 10 g/92 cal;   (Saturated Fat 1 g/13 cal);   Cholesterol 0 mg;
Sodium 1 mg;   Fiber 0 g;   Vitamin C 17% of Daily Value

MESCLUN LETTUCES
Calories 6;   Protein .5 g/2 cal;   Carbohydrates 1 g/3 cal;
Fat .1 g/1 cal;   (Saturated Fat 0 g/0 cal);   Cholesterol 0 mg;
Sodium 2 mg;   Fiber 0 g;   Vitamin A 9% of Daily Value

The smoked trout at Nora's comes from Mt. Walden, Virginia, a small country store with a big smoker in the back room. Richard Pla-Silva smokes trout and salmon with Virginia applewood. His trout is delicate and very moist.

Horseradish has big green leaves and long, white, spicy roots. I love its earthiness and sharpness. In Vienna fresh horseradish substitutes for mustard in many dishes. It is often mixed with grated apple and whipped cream to mellow it. At Nora's we mix horseradish with yogurt cheese for a low-fat alternative. To make yogurt cheese, line a colander with cheesecloth, pour in the yogurt, and allow it to drain 2 – 3 hours or overnight in the refrigerator.

Mesclun is a mix of different salad greens and herbs. It originated in the south of France, but is now commercially available in this country.

I like to make my own mix with baby lettuces and herbs, such as oakleaf, lolla rosa, radicchio, red mustard leaves, frisée, curly cress, small red chard leaves, basil, flat leaf parsley, and chervil.

Indonesian Quail Saté with Lemon Basmati Rice, Mustard Greens, Tomato Salad, Peanut Sauce, and Chili-Cucumber Relish

LEMON BASMATI RICE

Basmati is a long-grained rice originating in the Himalayan foothills. The grains, which are aged and dried, take on a wonderful perfumed aroma and nutty taste.

1 tablespoon canola oil
2 teaspoons minced shallots
½ teaspoon minced garlic
1¼ cups basmati rice

2¼ cups water
Sea salt and freshly ground black pepper
1 tablespoon lemon juice
Grated peel of 1 lemon, minced

Pour the oil into a medium saucepan and sauté the shallots and garlic until soft, about 3 minutes. Add the rice and stir, sautéing until well coated with oil. Add the water and salt and pepper to taste. Bring to a boil and stir. Reduce the heat, cover, and simmer for 15 – 17 minutes. Remove from the heat, uncover, and stir in the lemon juice and grated lemon zest.

Greens are high in Vitamin A, calcium, and iron and low in calories. I love greens and serve them often, especially in the fall and winter. The stems or stalks cut crosswise make a crunchy addition to a stir-fry and can even be pickled. Leaves can be stuffed with rice, raisins, nuts, and even ground lamb, like Greek stuffed grape leaves. I can find such a variety of greens in the market these days. In addition to the usual spinach, chard, collards, mustard, and beet, there are new Asian varieties such as mizuna, tat soi, and pak choi.

½ pound mustard greens, kale, Swiss chard, or spinach, washed and stems removed

1 teaspoon olive oil
Salt and freshly ground black pepper

Steam the greens in a medium saucepan using a collapsible steamer insert or blanch them in a non-reactive saucepan until bright green. Drain and toss with olive oil and season to taste with salt and pepper.

TOMATO SALAD

1 pound tomatoes, red and ripe
½ red onion, peeled and chopped
2 tablespoons chopped cilantro

1 tablespoon red wine vinegar
3 tablespoons olive oil
Sea salt and freshly ground black pepper

Cut the tomatoes in half and squeeze out the seeds. Cut into 1-inch cubes. Put the tomatoes, red onion, and cilantro into a small bowl. Add the vinegar and olive oil, season to taste with salt and pepper, and stir to mix.

In the fall and winter, we get tomatoes from Hummingbird Farm, on the eastern shore of Maryland. Raised in hydroponic greenhouses, these tomatoes are beautiful and taste much better than any other tomatoes I can buy at that time of year.

PEANUT SAUCE ✳

1 cup raw peanuts or cashews
1 stalk lemongrass, chopped or the peel of
    1 lemon
2 – 3-inch piece ginger, peeled and sliced
    across the grain
1/4 cup water

1 tablespoon tamari
Juice of 1 lemon
1/2 teaspoon ground cumin
Freshly ground black pepper

Preheat the oven to 350° F.

    Lay the nuts in a single layer on a sheet pan and roast for 8 – 10 minutes, until golden and toasted. Shake the pan from time to time. Remove from the oven and let cool.

    Put the peanuts or cashews, lemongrass or lemon peel, and ginger in the bowl of a food processor and process until ground into a butter. Add the water, tamari, lemon juice, and cumin. Purée until smooth and creamy. Season to taste with black pepper. Set aside.

You can make a shortcut version of this peanut sauce by starting with commercial peanut butter and adding ginger, tamari, and chili peppers.

Peanut sauce is also good with grilled vegetables.

Nuts are high in flavor, high in minerals and protein but, unfortunately, also high in fat and calories. At Nora's, I buy raw nuts and dry roast them myself to avoid adding extra fat.

CHILI-CUCUMBER RELISH ✳

1 medium cucumber (3/4 pound), peeled,
    seeded, and cut into chunks
1 jalapeño chili pepper, stemmed and sliced
1/2 green pepper, seeded and coarsely chopped
3 green onions, trimmed and coarsely chopped

4 tablespoons chopped cilantro or flat leaf parsley
1 tablespoon rice wine vinegar
Sea salt and freshly ground black pepper

Put the cucumber, chili, green pepper, green onions, cilantro or parsley, and vinegar into the bowl of a food processor. Process until the mixture has the consistency of a fine relish. Season to taste with salt and black pepper.

Add yogurt to this relish and you have raita, an Indian yogurt sauce, traditionally served with curry.

Indonesian saté is popular at Nora's. I make it with chicken or shrimp, or pork and lamb legs or shoulders. I like this marinade. Because it does not include peanuts, it is not so rich and high in fat. It is high in sodium because of the tamari, but keep in mind that you don't eat the marinade.

The seeds from broccoli rape are pressed into rapeseed oil, better known as canola oil, which has more cholesterol-balancing monounsaturated fat than any other oil except olive.

Marinate the quail overnight, if possible.

4 tablespoons canola oil
4 tablespoons lemon juice
4 tablespoons tamari
4 cloves garlic, chopped
1 medium onion, chopped
1 — 2 jalapeño chilies, chopped
½ cup cilantro leaves, tightly packed

5-inch piece lemon grass, chopped (optional)
1 teaspoon sesame oil
1½ teaspoons ground ginger
1 tablespoon brown sugar or blackstrap molasses

8 quail, split in half or whole, preferably boned
4 large cherry tomatoes, cut in half and scooped out (optional)
Cilantro sprigs for garnish

Preheat the grill or broiler.

Put the oil, lemon juice, tamari, garlic, onion, chilies, cilantro, lemon grass, sesame oil, ginger, and sugar or molasses in a blender. Purée until smooth. Put the quail in a glass baking dish and pour the marinade over them. Cover and marinate for at least 2 hours, preferably overnight.

Grill the quail, beginning with breast-side-down, 4 — 5 minutes each side or until the flesh turns opaque.

ASSEMBLY: Spoon some peanut sauce into 4 tomato halves and cucumber relish into the other 4 tomato halves. This step is optional; you can also serve the relishes directly on the plate or in small ramekins on the side.

Pile two grilled quail on each of 4 warmed plates. Arrange a spoonful of lemon basmati rice, greens and tomato salad in a semi-circle around the quail. Put the tomatoes on either side of the quail and garnish with sprigs of cilantro.

LEMON BASMATI RICE (1 CUP)
Calories 292;   Protein 22 cal;   Carbohydrates 222 cal;
Fat 48 cal;   (Saturated Fat 8 cal);   Cholesterol 0 mg;
Sodium 7 mg;   Fiber 1 g;   Vitamin C 6% of Daily Value

CHILI CUCUMBER RELISH PER SERVING
Calories 28;   Protein 3 cal;   Carbohydrates 23 cal;
Fat 2 cal;   (Saturated Fat 0 cal);   Cholesterol 0 mg;
Sodium 107 mg;   Fiber 1 g;   Vitamin C 54% of Daily Value

SATÉ MARINADE
Calories 206;   Protein 14 cal;   Carbohydrates 58 cal;
Fat 134 cal;   (Saturated Fat 10 cal);   Cholesterol 0 mg;
Sodium 1224 mg;   Fiber 1 g;   Iron 31% of Daily Value

INDONESIAN QUAIL
Calories 242;   Protein 161 cal;   Carbohydrates 5 cal;
Fat 76 cal;   (Saturated Fat 22 cal);   Cholesterol 0 mg;
Sodium 96 mg;   Fiber 0 g;   Iron 56% of Daily Value

PEANUT SAUCE (1.5 OUNCES)
Calories 169;   Protein 18 cal;   Carbohydrates 16 cal;
Fat 119 cal;   (Saturated Fat 16 cal);   Cholesterol 0 mg;
Sodium 132 mg;   Fiber 2 g;   Iron 15% of Daily Value

MUSTARD GREENS
Calories 26;   Protein 6 cal;   Carbohydrates 8 cal;
Fat 12 cal;   (Saturated Fat 2 cal);   Cholesterol 0 mg;
Sodium 45 mg;   Fiber 1 g;   Vitamin A 47% of Daily Value

TOMATO SALAD
Calories 136;   Protein 6 cal;   Carbohydrates 39 cal;
Fat 95 cal;   (Saturated Fat 13 cal);   Cholesterol 0 mg;
Sodium 13 mg;   Fiber 2 g

CHOCOLATE SORBET* WITH RASPBERRIES

You will need an ice cream maker.

3 cups water
1 cup sugar
1 tablespoon cocoa powder
8 ounces bittersweet or semi-sweet good quality chocolate

2 tablespoons Kahlúa or other liqueur

1 pint raspberries, washed and drained
Mint for garnish

I think chocolate sorbet is a good compromise, instead of chocolate ice cream. No cream, fewer calories and less fat.
I also like to make coconut sorbet instead of ice cream.

Pour the water, sugar, and cocoa powder into a medium saucepan and stir to dissolve. Bring the syrup to a boil. Remove the pan from the heat, add the chocolate and liqueur, and stir to melt the chocolate. Refrigerate the sorbet base to cool.

Follow manufacturer's directions for making sorbet in an ice cream machine. Store in freezer.

ASSEMBLY: Put a generous scoop of chocolate sorbet in the center of 4 dinner plates. Surround with raspberries. Garnish with mint.

CHOCOLATE SORBET (1 OUNCE)
Calories 84;   Protein 1 g/4 cal;   Carbohydrates 12 g/48 cal;
Fat 5 g/46 cal;   (Saturated Fat 2 g/18 cal);   Cholesterol 0 mg;
Sodium 1 mg;   Fiber 1 g;   Iron 3% of Daily Value

RASPBERRIES
Calories 33;   Protein .5 g/2 cal;   Carbohydrates 7 g/28 cal;
Fat .3 g/3 cal;   (Saturated Fat 0 g/0 cal);   Cholesterol 0 mg;
Sodium 0 mg;   Fiber 3 g;   Vitamin C 25% of Daily Value

AUTUMN MENU V

SEA SCALLOP SEVICHE WITH CHERRY TOMATOES AND ARUGULA

ROMAINE WITH GRILLED RED ONION, FETA CHEESE, BLACK OLIVES, AND RED WINE VINAIGRETTE

LEG OF LAMB ROAST WITH ROSEMARY SAUCE, ROASTED SWEET POTATOES, AND SUGAR SNAPS

BAKED APPLE WITH RAISIN-NUT STUFFING AND CARAMEL SAUCE

WINE SELECTIONS

*Lamb roast and rosemary offer rich flavors. They are perfect paired with a soft
Côte Rotie or a rich Hermitage. Red wine and lamb are a traditional combination.*

Côte Rotie 1989 Michel Ogier

Hermitage 1989 Paul Jaboulet

SEA SCALLOP SEVICHE❖
WITH CHERRY TOMATOES AND ARUGULA

Marinate the scallops overnight, if possible.

1 pound sea scallops
Juice of 3 limes
Grated peel of 1 lime
1 serrano or jalapeño chili, seeds removed,
    thinly sliced

2 tablespoons minced cilantro
¹⁄₂ teaspoon ground cumin
2 green onions, trimmed and chopped
Sea salt and freshly ground black pepper
1 teaspoon olive oil (optional)
¹⁄₄ pound cherry tomatoes
Arugula or other greens for garnish

Seviche appeared on Restaurant Nora's first menu 16 years ago and remains a mainstay. It is low-fat and very refreshing. It originated in Latin America where it is made with firm, white-fleshed fish. I also like to make it with shrimp and squid.

Rinse the scallops in cold water and remove the tough foot. If the scallops are very large, slice them horizontally into ¹⁄₂-inch rounds, otherwise leave them whole. Put them in a medium, non-reactive bowl, and add the lime juice to cover. Marinate the scallops in the refrigerator for 3 – 4 hours, preferably overnight. They should be opaque and "cooked" through.

    Drain off and discard all but 2 tablespoons of the accumulated juice. Add grated lime peel, the chili, cilantro, cumin, and green onions, stirring to combine. Season to taste with salt and pepper. Add a small amount of olive oil to balance the seviche if it is too acidic.

    ASSEMBLY: Spoon some of the seviche onto each of 4 luncheon plates. Garnish with arugula and cherry tomatoes.

If you want to make the seviche more substantial, add avocado, capers, and thinly sliced red onions.

SEA SCALLOP SEVICHE WITH CHERRY
TOMATOES AND ARUGULA
Calories 119;   Protein 20 g/80 cal;   Carbohydrates 8 g/30 cal;
Fat 1 g/9 cal;   (Saturated Fat .1 g/1 cal);   Cholesterol 37 mg;
Sodium 301 mg;   Fiber 1 g;   Iron 9% of Daily Value

ROMAINE WITH GRILLED RED ONIONS, FETA CHEESE, BLACK OLIVES, AND RED WINE VINAIGRETTE*

This salad makes a good base for a Greek chef's salad. Just add cooked chicken or lamb, sliced cucumbers, tomatoes, and peppers to the recipe.

Oregano is one of the few herbs I prefer to use dry because it tends to be bitter and harsh when fresh. I find it sweeter and more fragrant in the dried form.

1 small red onion, cut in ¼-inch slices
1 teaspoon olive oil

½ teaspoon red wine
1 teaspoon red wine vinegar
1 tablespoon olive oil
1 teaspoon dried oregano

Sea salt and freshly ground black pepper

1 head Romaine, washed, spun dry, and cut into 2-inch slices
2 ounces feta cheese, cut into ¼-inch cubes
16 – 20 black olives, Kalamata or Moroccan, pitted (optional)

Preheat the grill or broiler.

Brush the onion slices with olive oil and grill or broil until marked by the grill or browned from the broiler.

Put the wine, vinegar, olive oil, oregano, and salt and pepper into a small bowl. Whisk to combine. Toss the romaine with just enough dressing to lightly coat the leaves. If any dressing remains, reserve it for another use.

ASSEMBLY: Divide the romaine among 4 luncheon plates, top with a few red onion rings and sprinkle with feta cubes and olives.

ROMAINE WITH GRILLED RED ONIONS, FETA CHEESE, BLACK OLIVES, AND RED WINE VINAIGRETTE

Calories 108;   Protein 3 g/11 cal;   Carbohydrates 4 g/16 cal;
Fat 9 g/81 cal;   (Saturated Fat 1 g/8 cal);   Cholesterol 12 mg;
Sodium 427 mg;   Fiber 1 g;   Vitamin A 9% of Daily Value

Leg of Lamb Roast with Rosemary Sauce, Roasted Sweet Potatoes, and Sugar Snaps

Leg of Lamb ✳

The leg of lamb can be boned, seasoned, and tied the day before roasting.

4 – 5 anchovy fillets
2 tablespoons minced garlic
3 tablespoons rosemary needles
2 tablespoons olive oil
Freshly ground black pepper
1 small leg of lamb, about 3 pounds, boned or butterflied with bones reserved

1 carrot, coarsely chopped
1 stalk celery, coarsely chopped
1 small onion, coarsely chopped
1 small tomato, coarsely chopped
¼ cup water
1 cup red or white wine
2 teaspoons Dijon mustard
Rosemary sprigs for garnish

If you want a simpler version of this recipe, season the butterflied leg with the anchovies, garlic, rosemary, and pepper and omit the step of rolling and tying the lamb into a roast. Place the lamb on a preheated grill or under a broiler and cook for 10 – 15 minutes per side or until medium rare. Slice in long strips before serving.

Preheat the oven to 375° F.

Finely chop the anchovy, garlic, and 2 tablespoons of the rosemary by hand or in a mini-chopper. Put this mixture in a small bowl, add the olive oil and pepper, and stir to combine. Spread some of this seasoning on the boned side of the lamb and roll it up and tie it at regular intervals. Spread the remaining mixture on the outside of the lamb roast.

Scatter the lamb bones, carrot, celery, onion, and tomato on the bottom of a roasting pan. Add the water. Put the lamb on top and roast for 35 – 45 minutes, until the internal temperature is 130° F for medium rare (pink), or 140° F for medium.

Remove the lamb from the roasting pan and keep it warm by covering it with aluminum foil. Discard the bones and the vegetables. Pour off as much fat as possible from the roasting pan, leaving the accumulated meat juices.

Put the roasting pan over medium heat and add the wine, deglazing the pan by scraping all the browned and caramelized juices from the bottom and mixing them with the wine. Strain this liquid into a small saucepan, bring it to a boil, and whisk in the mustard and the remaining rosemary, stirring to combine. Taste and adjust the seasoning.

Leftover roasted sweet potatoes make a great salad when tossed with a mustard dressing (page 181). You can also mash them, add some sautéed onions, and make a delicious sweet potato pancake.

1½ pounds sweet potatoes, or Jewell yams peeled and cut into 2-inch chunks

1 tablespoon olive oil
Sea salt and freshly ground pepper

Put the yams in a medium bowl, add the olive oil, salt and pepper to taste. Toss to coat. After the lamb has been cooking for 15 minutes, add the yams to the same roasting pan if you have room, or to another roasting pan, and roast along with the lamb, for 30 – 40 minutes, until browned and soft.

SUGAR SNAPS

Sugar snap peas are eaten whole. When they are very fresh you can eat them raw. They make a delicious appetizer dipped in a spicy salsa, hummus, or peanut sauce.

½ pound sugar snaps, strings removed
1 teaspoon olive oil

Sea salt and freshly ground black pepper

Steam the sugar snaps in a small saucepan using a collapsible steamer or blanch them in boiling water. Drain, toss with the olive oil, and season to taste with salt and pepper.

ASSEMBLY: Place 3 or 4 slices of lamb on each of 4 dinner plates and spoon some rosemary sauce over the meat. Put a large spoonful of sugar snaps and roasted sweet potatoes next to the meat. Garnish with rosemary sprigs.

LEG OF LAMB WITH ROSEMARY SAUCE
Calories 540;   Protein 72 g/286 cal;   Carbohydrates 10 g/40 cal;
Fat 24 g/214 cal;   (Saturated Fat 7 g/59 cal);   Cholesterol 156 mg;
Sodium 533 mg;   Fiber 2 g;   Iron 38% of Daily Value

ROASTED SWEET POTATOES (6 OUNCES)
Calories 200;   Protein 3 g/12 cal;   Carbohydrates 47 g/188 cal;
Fat 1 g/10 cal;   (Saturated Fat 0 g/0 cal);   Cholesterol 0 mg.
Sodium 14 mg;   Fiber 4 g;   Vitamin C 34% of Daily Value

SUGAR SNAPS
Calories 34;   Protein 2 g/7 cal;   Carbohydrates 4 g/16 cal;
Fat 1 g/11 cal;   (Saturated Fat .2 g/2 cal);   Cholesterol 0 mg;
Sodium 2 mg;   Fiber 2 g;   Vitamin C 45% of Daily Value

BAKED APPLE WITH
RAISIN-NUT STUFFING AND CARAMEL SAUCE

4 large, tart cooking apples such as Gala or
    Granny Smith
¼ cup raisins
½ cup chopped walnuts
1 tablespoon brown sugar

2 tablespoons softened butter
1 cup water or apple cider
Caramel sauce (page 178)
Fresh mint for garnish

This is an easy fall dessert. Leftovers served with yogurt are great for breakfast.

At Nora's, we serve baked apples with savory stuffings such as Vermont cheddar and wild rice or corn bread and Monterey Jack cheese for our daily vegetarian plate.

Preheat the oven to 350° F.

Remove the apple cores with a corer or vegetable peeler.

Make a paste by mixing the raisins, chopped walnuts, sugar, and butter by hand or in a mini chopper. Form this stuffing into a cylinder and stuff as much as you can into the hollowed-out core of each apple.

Put the apples into a baking pan and add enough water or cider to cover the bottom of the pan, about ¼ -inch deep. Bake for 45 – 60 minutes, or until the apples are cooked through and can be easily pierced with a knife.

ASSEMBLY: Pour some of the caramel sauce onto the center of each dessert plate. Place a baked apple in the middle and garnish with a sprig of mint.

BAKED APPLE WITH STUFFING
Calories 295;   Protein 3 g/11 cal;   Carbohydrates 36 g/144 cal;
Fat 16 g/140 cal;   (Saturated Fat 5 g/41 cal);   Cholesterol 16 mg;
Sodium 64 mg;   Fiber 4 g;   Vitamin C 14% of Daily Value

AUTUMN MENU VI

AUTUMN VEGETARIAN PLATE

GRILLED PORTOBELLO MUSHROOM WITH GOAT CHEESE AND CORN RELISH

SAFFRON FETTUCCINE WITH TEN KINDS OF TOMATOES, FRESH MOZZARELLA, BASIL, AND EXTRA-VIRGIN OLIVE OIL VINAIGRETTE

WINE SELECTIONS

The ten varieties of tomatoes, with all their acidity, offer a challenge to wine. In this case, they are well matched with a clean, crisp Sancerre or Sauvignon Blanc.

Chateau St. Jean 1991 Sauvignon Blanc

Sancerre Lucian Thomas 1991 France

GRILLED PORTOBELLO MUSHROOM WITH
GOAT CHEESE AND CORN RELISH

*4 portobello mushrooms, about ½ pound,
   stemmed and wiped clean*
*Tamari-balsamic vinegar marinade
   (page 81)*

*4 ounces goat cheese, log-shaped, cut into 4
   rounds*

Preheat grill or broiler.

Brush the portobellos with the tamari-balsamic vinaigrette marinade. Grill or broil for 2 minutes on each side or until cooked through and softened.

ASSEMBLY: Put a portobello on each of 4 large dinner plates. Place a round of goat cheese in the center of each mushroom and spoon some corn-red pepper relish on top.

GRILLED PORTOBELLO MUSHROOM WITH GOAT
CHEESE AND CORN RELISH
Calories 98;   Protein 6 g/23 cal;   Carbohydrates 3 g/11 cal;
Fat 7 g/64 cal;   (Saturated Fat 4 g/33 cal);   Cholesterol 22 mg;
Sodium 145 mg;   Fiber 1 g;   Iron 4% Of Daily Value

Portobello mushrooms are adult crimini mushrooms, cousins of the common cultivated white mushroom. Grilled portobello mushrooms have a lot of flavor and texture. They taste nearly like meat and have become a bestseller at Nora's.

You can top each mushroom with mozzarella instead of goat cheese and broil them until the cheese melts. Try this grilled-cheese mushroom with my tomato salsa (page 110).

SAFFRON FETTUCCINE WITH TEN KINDS OF TOMATOES, FRESH MOZZARELLA, BASIL, AND BALSAMIC VINAIGRETTE

True Italian mozzarella is made in the southern regions of the country from water buffalo milk. Nowadays, most American mozzarella is made from cow's milk.

10 kinds of tomatoes with fresh basil and balsamic vinaigrette (page 74)
4 ounces fresh mozzarella, cut in ¼-inch cubes

Saffron fettuccine (page 99)
1 teaspoon olive oil
Basil leaves for garnish

Make the tomato salad according to the recipe on page 74. Add the mozzarella.

Make the saffron fettuccine following the recipe on page 99, cutting the pasta into fettuccine noodles.

Bring a large pot of water to a boil. Add the saffron fettuccine and cook for 3 – 4 minutes, until al dente. Drain in a colander.

Toss the pasta with 1 teaspoon olive oil to prevent it from sticking. Mix the 10 kinds of tomatoes with the basil and balsamic vinaigrette.

ASSEMBLY: Put the fettuccine noodles on 4 large, warmed dinner plates. Arrange several spoonfuls of the tomato–basil salad on top.

Autumn/Winter Vegetarian Menu Suggestions

Pumpkin Soup with Pepitas (page 123)
Caesar Salad with Farm Eggs and Garlic Croutons (page 190)
Wild Mushroom Risotto with Spinach (page 20)
Pears Poached in Sauternes with Chocolate Sauce and Whipped Cream (page 121)

Clear Wild Mushroom Soup (page 163)
Radicchio and Watercress Salad with
Herbed Goat Cheese Toast and Sherry Vinaigrette (page 22)
Roasted Winter Vegetables with Garlic, Rosemary, and Lemon (page 192)
Kheer (Indian Creamed Rice) (page 168)

Yam and Leek Soup with Garlic Croutons (page 87)
Belgian Endive, Mâche, Beets, Apples, and Walnut Oil Dressing (page 154)
Saffron Fettuccine with Sundried Tomato Pesto,
Broccoli, Greens, and Carrots (page 157)
Orange-Grand Marnier Cake with Chocolate Sorbet (page 194)

Chanterelle Mushroom-Leek Bruschetta with Balsamic Vinegar (page 117)
Spinach and Frisée Salad with Baby Beets and Mustard Vinaigrette (page 58-59)
Indonesian Vegetable Saté with Peanut Sauce,
Basmati Rice, Raita, and Greens (page 136)
Caramelized Bananas with Lime Tequila Ice Cream and Chocolate Sauce (page 187)

WINTER

WINTER MENU I

SOUTHWESTERN BEEF TARTARE WITH LIME, CHILIES, CILANTRO, AND FLOUR TORTILLAS

BELGIAN ENDIVE, MÂCHE, BEETS, AND APPLES WITH WALNUTS AND SHERRY VINAIGRETTE

GRILLED WHOLE ROCKFISH WITH SUNDRIED TOMATO PESTO, GRILLED POLENTA, AND BROCCOLI RAPE

CHOCOLATE PECAN CAKE WITH BOURBON CREAM

WINE SELECTIONS

This menu, with rockfish and sundried tomato pesto, calls for Chardonnay.
The pesto goes well with so many flavors. A fruit flavored California Chardonnay would be the wine of choice.

Au Bon Climat 1990 Santa Barbara County

Hess Collection 1990 Napa Valley

Southwestern Beef Tartare with Lime, Chilies, Cilantro, and Flour Tortillas

Twelve 6-inch flour tortillas
1 pound beef, preferably sirloin or round
2 teaspoons lime juice
½ cup chopped cilantro leaves, loosely
  packed
1 jalapeño chili, seeded and minced

½ teaspoon ground cumin
1 teaspoon ancho chili powder (optional)
Sea salt and freshly ground black pepper
Cilantro sprigs for garnish
Red, yellow, and green whole chilies for garnish
Lime wedges for garnish

Preheat the oven to 375° F.

Assemble the steak tartare at most 15 minutes before serving because the lime juice cooks the meat and will turn it gray if mixed too far in advance. You can prepare all the ingredients ahead and mix them together at the last minute.

Grind the meat in a food processor or a meat grinder until finely chopped. Put the meat in a bowl and add the lime juice, cilantro, chili, cumin, the optional chili powder, and salt and pepper to taste. Mix well with a fork. Make four 3-inch patties with the seasoned meat and score each patty in a decorative pattern using a knife blade.

Wrap the tortillas in aluminum foil and bake for 4 minutes, or until warm. You can also heat the tortillas in a dry sauté pan or on a preheated grill just until softened. Fold into quarters.

ASSEMBLY: Put a steak tartare patty on the side of each of 4 dinner plates. Arrange 3 folded tortillas on the opposite side of each plate. Garnish with sprigs of cilantro, a wedge of lime, and red, yellow, and green whole chilies.

SOUTHWESTERN BEEF TARTARE
Calories 422;   Protein 20 g/78 cal;   Carbohydrates 57 g/226 cal;
Fat 14 g/128 cal;   (Saturated Fat 5 g/46 cal);   Cholesterol 32 mg;
Sodium 383 mg;   Fiber 4 g;   Vitamin C 86% of Daily Value

If you like your steak tartare spicier, add more chili pepper.

Beefsteak tartare originated in Russia, where the Tartars eat their meat raw, shredded with a knife. Usually the meat is seasoned with capers, onions, and parsley, shaped into a mound, and topped with a raw egg yolk.

Sometimes I make an Ethiopian tartare adding a spice mixture called Berbere to the meat, serving it with Ingera, the pancake-like bread Ethiopians use to pick up their food.

Belgian Endive, Mâche, Beets, and Apples with Walnuts and Sherry Vinaigrette

*To clean Belgian endive you
need only to wipe the outside
leaves with a damp cloth. It is
not necessary to wash them since
endive is grown in sand,
not dirt.*

*When you cut endive, use a
stainless steel knife—carbon
knives discolor the leaves.*

¹/₄ cup English walnut halves
8 small beets (about ¹/₂ pound)
4 heads Belgian endive
4 – 6 ounces mâche or watercress, washed
  and spun dry

Sherry vinaigrette (page 22)
1 apple, thinly sliced

Preheat the oven to 350° F.

Steam the beets for 12 – 15 minutes in a small, covered saucepan using a collapsible steamer. Allow to cool.

Put the walnuts on a baking sheet and bake for 8 – 10 minutes, until fragrant and toasted. Peel and quarter the cooked beets. Wipe the outside of the Belgian endive with a damp cloth, trim the base, and separate the leaves.

Assembly: Just before serving, toss the mâche or watercress with some of the sherry vinaigrette. Divide the greens among the 4 plates, placing them in the center of each dinner plate. Arrange the Belgian endive and the apple slices around the edge of the greens. Add beets to each salad and sprinkle with the walnuts. Drizzle the remaining sherry vinaigrette over the endive leaves.

BELGIAN ENDIVE MÂCHE SALAD
Calories 122;   Protein 4 g/17 cal;   Carbohydrates 15 g/60 cal;
Fat 5 g/45 cal;   (Saturated Fat .3 g/3 cal);   Cholesterol 0 mg;
Sodium 69 mg;   Fiber 6 g;   Vitamin A 32% of Daily Value

GRILLED WHOLE ROCKFISH WITH SUNDRIED TOMATO PESTO, GRILLED POLENTA, AND BROCCOLI RAPE

SUNDRIED TOMATO PESTO *

3 ounces sundried tomatoes
1 tablespoon minced garlic
1/3 cup loosely packed basil leaves, julienned
1 tablespoon balsamic vinegar

2 tablespoons olive oil
1 tablespoon pine nuts (optional)
2 tablespoons water
Sea salt and freshly ground black pepper

This recipe makes about 1 cup of pesto. I like to spread this pesto on toasted bread to make a bruschetta. I also use it as a sauce with a tubular pasta like rigatoni, and serve it with freshly grated Parmesan cheese.

Sundried tomatoes come dry-packed or oil-packed. If you are using dry-packed tomatoes, put them in a small strainer and dip them into boiling water for about 1 minute, until they are softened. Drain the softened tomatoes well before proceeding. This step is not necessary if you use tomatoes preserved in oil.

Put the tomatoes, garlic, basil, vinegar, olive oil, pinenuts, and water into the blender. Purée with an on and off motion until the mixture is chopped. Season to taste with salt and pepper.

ROSEMARY POLENTA *

4 teaspoons olive oil
1 teaspoon chopped shallots
1/2 teaspoon chopped garlic
2 1/4 cup water

1/2 teaspoon minced rosemary needles
1/2 teaspoon sea salt
Freshly ground black pepper
4 ounces instant Italian polenta

Sometimes we double the amount of liquid and serve a creamier polenta. Polenta is the Italian word for cornmeal mush. It is a staple in Northern Italy and eaten for breakfast, lunch, or dinner. If you cannot find instant polenta, use stone ground yellow cornmeal.

Put 3 teaspoons of the olive oil into a medium saucepan and sauté the shallots and garlic for 1 minute or until softened. Add the water, rosemary, and salt and pepper to taste. Bring to a boil and stir in the polenta. Stirring continuously, cook for 2 minutes or until all the water has been absorbed and the polenta is smooth.

Rinse an 8-inch square or loaf pan with cold water to prevent the polenta from sticking to it. Pour the polenta into the pan and smooth the surface with a wet spatula. Refrigerate. When the polenta is cool and firm, unmold it and cut it into 2 – 3-inch wide strips.

Preheat the grill or broiler.

Brush the polenta with the remaining olive oil and grill 2 – 3 minutes per side until warmed through and marked by the grill. Cut the polenta into wedges or triangles and keep warm in a slow oven.

The proportion for 4 people is 1 1/2 cups cornmeal to 6 cups water. Bring the water to a boil and add the cornmeal in a thin stream, stirring constantly with a wire wisk to avoid lumps. Add 1 1/2 tablespoons olive oil and 1 tablespoon salt to the cornmeal and cook about 20 minutes, until the mixture is smooth and thick. You can flavor the polenta by adding chopped fresh herbs, grilled onions, olive oil, grated cheese, or butter. I especially like to add cracked black pepper.

*I find whole, small grilled fish
with head and bones intact,
much juicier than fillets
or steaks.*

*Rockfish used to be plentiful in
the Chesapeake Bay until over-
fishing and pollution drastically
reduced their numbers. We buy
farmed rockfish from the Eastern
Shore of the Chesapeake Bay.*

*Broccoli rape, also called raab
or rapini, (and pronounced
RAH-pay) is related to cabbage
and turnip. It is a leafy green
with broccoli-like buds and a
pungent bitter flavor. It is more
popular in Italy than in the
United States.*

*Four 1 — 1¼-pound whole rockfish, scaled,
gutted, and cleaned or four 6-ounce
rockfish fillets*

*2 tablespoons olive oil
Sea salt and freshly ground black pepper
¾ pound broccoli rape, trimmed*

Preheat the grill or broiler.

Brush the whole rockfish or fillets with 1 tablespoon of the olive oil and sea-son to taste with salt and pepper.

Grill or broil whole rockfish for 6 — 8 minutes on the first side, until the flesh in the stomach cavity turns opaque. Turn and grill or broil the other side about 6 minutes. If you are using fillets, put the skin side of the fillet toward the heat source. Fillets take less time to cook than the whole fish, about 4 min-utes each side.

Blanch the broccoli rape in boiling water or steam it in a medium saucepan using a collapsible steamer until tender and bright green, 3 — 4 minutes. Drain and toss with 1 tablespoon of the olive oil. Season to taste with salt and pepper.

Assembly: Divide the broccoli rape among 4 warm, preferably oval, dinner plates. Place one whole rockfish or one fillet on top of the greens on each plate. Add a spoonful of sundried tomato pesto and 3 or 4 triangles of grilled polenta to the side of each plate.

SUNDRIED TOMATO PESTO
Calories 139;   Protein 3 g/11 cal;   Carbohydrates 17 g/66 cal;
Fat 7 g/62 cal;   (Saturated Fat 1 g/9 cal);   Cholesterol 0 mg;
Sodium 27 mg;   Fiber 1 g;   Vitamin A 110% of Daily Value

POLENTA
Calories 146;   Protein 3 g/10 cal;   Carbohydrates 23 g/91 cal;
Fat 5 g/45 cal;   (Saturated Fat .7 g/6 cal);   Cholesterol 0 mg;
Sodium 272 mg;   Fiber 2 g;   Iron 7% of Daily Value

GRILLED ROCKFISH
Calories 193;   Protein 24 g/95 cal;   Carbohydrates 5 g/19 cal;
Fat 9 g/79 cal;   (Saturated Fat 1 g/13 cal);   Cholesterol 39 mg;
Sodium 91 mg;   Fiber 2 g;   Iron 7% of Daily Value

CHOCOLATE PECAN CAKE WITH BOURBON CREAM

CHOCOLATE PECAN CAKE *

1 ½ cups pecans
4 ounces unsalted butter
4 ounces semi-sweet chocolate
¾ cup sugar

6 egg yolks
¾ cup bread crumbs
6 egg whites

Preheat the oven to 325° F.

Spread the pecans onto a baking sheet and bake for 8 – 10 minutes, until fragrant and toasted. Let the nuts cool. Coarsely chop the pecans.

Butter an 8-inch springform pan with one teaspoon of butter and dust with some of the bread crumbs.

Melt the chocolate in a double-boiler over simmering water. Remove from the heat and allow to cool slightly.

Combine the butter, sugar, and cooled, melted chocolate in the bowl of a mixer and beat until the batter changes to a lighter color and becomes creamy, about 5 minutes. Scrape down the sides of the bowl once or twice while beating.

Add the egg yolks, one at a time, and continue beating. Lower the speed of the mixer and add the ground pecans and bread crumbs.

Beat egg whites until soft but not stiff. Stir a third of the beaten whites into the batter, blending thoroughly. Gently fold in remaining whites, working quickly and carefully to incorporate all the whites without deflating the batter.

Pour the batter into the prepared pan and smooth the top. Bake 50 – 55 minutes or until a toothpick inserted in the center comes out clean.

Allow the cake to cool in the pan for 10 minutes before turning it out onto a cake rack. Let the cake cool completely before adding the glaze. Serves 12.

This is my grandmother's recipe for a traditional Austrian cake, called Rehrücken. The name means "venison saddle" because the cake is usually baked in a long, half-roll pan.

No matter what you do, this cake never fails. Underbaked, it tastes like a brownie. The original Viennese recipe uses almonds. Sometimes, I make an Italian version, substituting pine nuts and serving it with an Amaretto cream.

It is important not to overbeat the egg whites. Whip them just until they keep their shape. If over-beaten, they are difficult to fold in thoroughly and over-beaten whites can cause the cake to rise too high, crack, and fall as it cools.

CHOCOLATE GLAZE ✻

For one 8-inch cake

3 ounces semi-sweet chocolate

3 ounces unsalted butter, softened
1 ounce of room temperature milk chocolate for garnish

Melt the semi-sweet chocolate in a double boiler over simmering water. Add the butter and stir until blended and smooth. Remove the glaze from the heat and allow it to cool and thicken to the consistency of thick cream.

Brush the cake to remove any loose crumbs, and place both the cake and the cooling rack on a sheet pan to catch the chocolate glaze. Slowly pour a pool of chocolate glaze onto the center of the cake. Working from the center out, use a long metal spatula to spread the glaze evenly over the top and sides of the cake.

For a smoother look, you can glaze the cake a second time. Scoop the excess glaze from the sheet pan and reheat it in a small double boiler. Pour it through a sieve, if necessary to remove any cake crumbs, and cool it slightly to thicken a bit. Pour the glaze again onto the center of the cake and allow it to spread without using a spatula.

With a vegetable peeler, shave off some curls of the milk chocolate and sprinkle them on top of the cake. Allow the glaze to set for 2 hours at room temperature or 20 minutes in the refrigerator.

BOURBON LIGHT WHIPPED CREAM

4 tablespoons heavy cream
1 egg white
1 tablespoon bourbon

1 tablespoon superfine or confectioners' sugar
Fresh mint for garnish

Whip the egg white until it holds its shape. Whip the cream in a separate bowl until it forms soft peaks, then add the sugar and bourbon. Continue to whip the cream until it forms soft peaks again. Fold the cream into the egg white.

ASSEMBLY: Cut 4 pieces of the cake and put one piece on each of 4 dessert plates. Garnish with a dollop of bourbon light whipped cream and a sprig of mint.

CHOCOLATE PECAN CAKE
Calories 298;   Protein 5 g/19 cal;   Carbohydrates 22 g/89 cal;
Fat 21 g/190 cal;   (Saturated Fat 6 g/57 cal);   Cholesterol 127 mg;
Sodium 96 mg;   Fiber 1 g;   Vitamin A 6% of Daily Value

CHOCOLATE GLAZE
Calories 89;   Protein .5 g/2 cal;   Carbohydrates 6 g/23 cal;
Fat 7 g/64 cal;   (Saturated Fat 4 g/32 cal);   Cholesterol 16 mg;
Sodium 6 mg;   Fiber 0 g;   Vitamin A 6% of Daily Value

BOURBON LIGHT WHIPPED CREAM
Calories 22;   Protein .5 g/2 cal;   Carbohydrates 1 g/3 cal;
Fat 2 g/17 cal;   (Saturated Fat 1 g/10 cal);   Cholesterol 7 mg;
Sodium 7 mg;   Fiber 0 g;   Vitamin A 3% of Daily Value

WINTER MENU II

CLEAR WILD MUSHROOM SOUP

ROASTED DOUBLE PORK CHOP WITH APPLE-HORSERADISH STUFFING, CALVADOS SAUCE, STEAMED BEETS AND THEIR
GREENS, AND BUTTERNUT SQUASH PURÉE

MÂCHE LETTUCE AND SHREDDED CARROT SALAD WITH LEMON-GARLIC DRESSING

INDIAN CREAMY RICE DESSERT WITH RAISINS AND ALMONDS

WINE SELECTIONS

*Pork and a red Syrah work so well together. The horseradish in this dish adds a very strong flavor
and the Syrah can stand up to it. A northern Rhone from France or a Californian Syrah would fit best.*

Saint Joseph 1989 Gonon, Rhone Valley

Qupe 1991 Central Coast, California

CLEAR WILD MUSHROOM SOUP*

1 1/2 tablespoons olive oil
2 tablespoons minced shallots
1 teaspoon minced garlic
1 small leek, white part only, thinly sliced
1 small carrot, peeled and chopped
2 ribs celery, chopped
3/4 pound assorted wild mushrooms such as
    chanterelle, hen of the woods, porcini,
    shiitake, crimini, or portobello

1 tablespoon tamari
3 cups chicken or vegetable stock or water with 2
    chicken bouillon cubes
Sea salt and freshly ground pepper
1 1/2 tablespoons chopped flat leaf parsley or
    tarragon for garnish

Heat the olive oil in a medium saucepan, add the shallots and garlic, and sauté
on a medium flame, stirring often, until soft, 4 – 5 minutes. Stir in the leek,
carrot, celery, and wild mushrooms and sauté until the mixture is softened, 4 – 5
minutes. Add the tamari, the stock or water with bouillon cubes and bring to a
boil. Reduce the heat, cover, and simmer about 20 minutes. Season to taste with
salt and pepper.

ASSEMBLY: Ladle the wild mushroom soup into 4 warm soup bowls. Sprinkle
with chopped parsley or tarragon.

This is Steven's favorite soup. We often make a creamed version of this soup at Nora's by puréeing it in the blender when we have accumulated enough trimmings and stems left over from our other wild mushroom dishes. This homey soup tastes just as good as the more elegant version and makes economical use of the flavorful trimmings.

To enhance the soup and give it a true woodsy flavor, cook some dried cèpes or porcini with the fresh mushrooms.

During World War II and afterwards, my parents leased a farm in Tyrol in the Austrian Alps, because there was more food available in the countryside and we could escape the bombings and destruction of Vienna. My grandmother, Omi, lived with us and I remember these as very happy years. Our favorite outing in the fall was to go wild mushroom hunting. Whatever "extra" mushrooms we found that we could not eat right away, Omi would slice thinly, thread on a long string, mount the string on a frame, and place it in the sun to dry. We had the most delicious wild mushroom soups during the winter months made from these dried mushrooms.

Roasted Double Pork Chops with Apple-Horseradish Stuffing,* Calvados Sauce, Steamed Beets and Their Greens, and Butternut Squash Purée

ROASTED DOUBLE PORK CHOPS WITH APPLE-HORSERADISH STUFFING*

You want to keep the opening of the pocket in the pork chop small to prevent the stuffing from oozing out. If you buy a pork chop that is completely split for stuffing, close it with skewers or toothpicks before roasting.

Try other stuffings for the pork chops like sauerkraut, cooked cabbage, cornbread with sausage, or wild rice with chestnuts. If you like your pork chops nice and brown, but you don't want to make a sauce, baste them with the following all-purpose glaze after they have roasted for about 10 minutes.

GLAZE*

1 tablespoon tamari
1 tablespoon balsamic vinegar
1 tablespoon olive oil
Freshly ground black pepper

3 tablespoons canola oil
2 tablespoons shallots
1 apple, washed and grated
2-inch piece horseradish, about 4 tablespoons grated

1 tablespoon Dijon mustard
Sea salt and freshly ground black pepper

4 pork chops, about 2 inches thick

Preheat oven to 350° F.

Heat 2 tablespoons canola oil in a small sauté pan and sauté shallots for 2 – 4 minutes. Add the apple and cook until softened, about 2 minutes. Remove from the heat, add the horseradish and mustard, and season to taste with salt and pepper.

Make a pocket in each pork chop with a paring knife by cutting a 2-inch incision in the side of the pork chop opposite the bone. Move the knife in an arc, back and forth, cutting a large interior pocket in the chop but keeping the opening small. This is where you will put the stuffing.

Push as much apple stuffing as you can into this pocket. The pork chop should look plump and rounded. Repeat with all of the chops.

Brush the chops with the remaining oil and season to taste with salt and pepper. Set them on a sheet or roasting pan and roast for about 30 minutes, until the chops and the stuffing are cooked through and a knife inserted next to the bone shows the meat to be pink.

1 teaspoon canola oil

2 tablespoons shallots

2 cups veal or chicken stock, or 1 chicken
    bouillon cube dissolved in 2 cups
    warm water

2 tablespoons Calvados or applejack

Sea salt and freshly ground black pepper

Heat the oil in a medium saucepan and sauté the shallots until soft, about 5 minutes. Add the stock or water and bouillon cube and bring to a boil. Reduce the heat and simmer for 30 minutes or until you reduce the sauce to about 1 cup. Add the Calvados or applejack, raise the heat and cook for 1 more minute to boil off some of the alcohol. Season to taste with salt and pepper.

You can also make a base for this sauce by puréeing 2 roasted shallots in a blender with 1 cup stock or water, the Calvados, salt, and pepper. Cook this over high heat for 1 – 2 minutes to boil off the alcohol.

Calvados is a distilled brandy made from apples. It comes from Normandy, France, where locals often indulge in a "trou Normand," a sip between courses to help digest their rich cuisine.

You can also roast the squash
before peeling. Cut each squash
in half, remove the seeds and
bake face-down on a baking
sheet at 350° F for 30 minutes
or until soft. Scoop out the pulp
with a large spoon and proceed
as directed. You can also substitute yams, pumpkin, or sweet
potatoes for the squash.

2 butternut squashes, about 1 1/2 pounds,
   peeled, seeded, and cut into 1-inch cubes
Pinch mace or allspice

Sea salt and freshly ground black pepper
2 pounds steamed beets or 1 1/2 pounds steamed
   beets and 1/2 pound steamed beet greens

Steam the squash for 20 minutes or until tender using a collapsible steamer
insert in a saucepan. Purée the squash in a food processor. Season to taste with
mace or allspice and salt and pepper. If the purée is too thick, add some water.

ASSEMBLY: Ladle some Calvados sauce on each of 4 warm dinner plates and
top with a pork chop. Surround the chop with the beets and their greens and a
big spoonful of butternut squash purée.

ROASTED DOUBLE PORK CHOP WITH
APPLE-HORSERADISH STUFFING
Calories 300;   Protein 25 g/101 cal;   Carbohydrates 10 g/39 cal;
Fat 18 g/160 cal;   (Saturated Fat 3 g/29 cal);   Cholesterol 58 mg;
Sodium 149 mg;   Fiber 1 g;   Iron 6% of Daily Value

PORK GLAZE (NORA'S NOTE)
Calories 41;   Protein .5 g/2 cal;   Carbohydrates 2 g/9 cal;
Fat 3 g/30 cal;   (Saturated Fat .4 g/4 cal);   Cholesterol 0 mg;
Sodium 253 mg;   Fiber 0 g;   Vitamin C 2% of Daily Value

CALVADOS SAUCE
Calories 24;   Protein .25 g/1 cal;   Carbohydrates 3 g/13 cal;
Fat 1 g/10 cal;   (Saturated Fat .1 g/1 cal);   Cholesterol 0 mg;
Sodium 4 mg;   Fiber 0 g;   Vitamin A 6% of Daily Value

BUTTERNUT SQUASH AND STEAMED BEETS
Calories 161;   Protein 4 g/16 cal;   Carbohydrates 35 g/141 cal;
Fat .4 g/4 cal;   (Saturated Fat .1 g/1 cal);   Cholesterol 0 mg;
Sodium 130 mg;   Fiber 8 g;   Vitamin A 119% of Daily Value

MÂCHE LETTUCE AND SHREDDED CARROT SALAD
WITH LEMON-GARLIC DRESSING

LEMON-GARLIC DRESSING*

This salad was inspired by Joel
Robuchon's Grated Carrot
Salad in Patricia Well's book,
Simply French. I lightened
the dressing by substituting
water for some of the oil. This
dressing also works well with
other root vegetables such
as parsnip and celeriac
(celery root).

2 tablespoons lemon juice
3 tablespoons olive oil
2 tablespoons water

3 large cloves garlic
Sea salt and freshly ground black pepper

Put the lemon juice, olive oil, water, garlic, and salt and pepper into the blender.
Purée until garlic is finely chopped.

MÂCHE LETTUCE AND SHREDDED CARROT* SALAD

1 large carrot, trimmed and peeled
½ pound mâche, washed and spun dry

1 teaspoon chopped flat leaf parsley for garnish
4 slices of lemon, for garnish

Grate the carrot with a hand grater or in a food processor. Mix it with 4 tablespoons of the lemon-garlic dressing and marinate for at least 1 hour or overnight in the refrigerator.

ASSEMBLY: Toss the mâche with the remaining lemon dressing. Arrange the lettuce on 4 luncheon plates, put the grated carrots in the center, and sprinkle with parsley. Garnish with a lemon slice.

LEMON-GARLIC DRESSING
Calories 67;   Protein .25 g/1 cal;   Carbohydrates 2 g/6 cal;
Fat 7 g/61 cal;   (Saturated Fat 1 g/9 cal);   Cholesterol 0 mg;
Sodium 1 mg;   Fiber 0 g;   Vitamin C 7% of Daily Value

MÂCHE AND SHREDDED CARROT SALAD
Calories 23;   Protein 1 g/5 cal;   Carbohydrates 4 g/16 cal;
Fat .2 g/2 cal;   (Saturated Fat 0 g/0 cal);   Cholesterol 0 mg;
Sodium 15 mg;   Fiber 2 gm;   Vitamin A 65% of Daily Value

Mâche, also called lamb's lettuce or corn salad, is a winter or early spring lettuce. In Austria, it is called Vogerl salad, or bird's salad. Perhaps this is because the leaves are small and delicate, just right for a bird! My mother used to combine mâche with potato salad made with new fingerling potatoes.

INDIAN CREAMY RICE DESSERT WITH RAISINS AND ALMONDS*

Arborio rice is a starchy, short grain rice from the Po river valley in northern Italy that is traditionally used to make risotto. Despite the unusually small proportion of rice to milk in this recipe, ⅓ cup arborio is enough to make this creamy dessert. If you must use another variety of rice, you will probably need to use more.

This is another example of the advantages of cross-cultural cooking. This creamy rice dessert comes from India where it is called kheer, but I use rice from Italy to make it.

1 quart milk
4 cardamom seed pods
1 cinnamon stick
2 cloves
⅓ cup arborio rice

2 tablespoons raisins
⅓ cup sugar

¼ cup or 20 whole almonds
Mint for garnish

Preheat the oven to 350° F.

Bring the milk, cardamom, cinnamon, and cloves to a boil. Add the rice, stir to combine, and return to a boil. Reduce the heat and simmer over very low heat for about 30 minutes, stirring from time to time. Don't cover. Add the raisins and sugar and simmer for another 45 minutes. Remove from the heat.

While the rice is cooking, put the almonds on a baking sheet and roast them in the oven for 10 minutes or until toasted and golden brown. Slice them into smaller pieces or chop in a food processor.

ASSEMBLY: Spoon creamy rice into each of 4 warm soup bowls, sprinkle with toasted almonds, and garnish with a sprig of mint. This dessert is also good cold.

CREAMY RICE DESSERT
Calories 297;   Protein 12 g/47 cal;   Carbohydrates 48 g/191 cal;
Fat 7 g/59 cal;   (Saturated Fat 2 g/18 cal);   Cholesterol 10 mg;
Sodium 130 mg;   Fiber 2 g;   Calcium 38% of Daily Value

WINTER MENU III

CHESAPEAKE BAY OYSTERS ON THE HALF SHELL WITH RASPBERRY MIGNONETTE

WARM FRISÉE, RADICCHIO, AND BACON SALAD WITH GARLIC-THYME VINAIGRETTE

CHICKEN AND CASHEW CURRY WITH BASMATI RICE, BROCCOLI, CHUTNEY, AND MINT RAITA

BITTERSWEET CHOCOLATE MOUSSE WITH CARAMEL SAUCE AND LEMON BALM

WINE SELECTIONS

Gewuürztraminer and curry is an exciting, mouth-filling combination.
We recommend either a full-bodied Alsatian or a leaner Californian Gewuürztraminer.

Lucian Albrecht 1990, Alsace

Chateau St. Jean 1990, Sonoma Valley

CHESAPEAKE BAY OYSTERS ON THE HALF SHELL WITH RASPBERRY MIGNONETTE

RASPBERRY MIGNONETTE

2 tablespoons raspberry vinegar
1 tablespoon finely minced shallots

Sea salt and freshly ground white pepper

Pour the vinegar into a small bowl, add the shallots, and stir to combine. Season to taste with salt and pepper.

OYSTERS ON THE HALF SHELL

20 — 24 oysters

Cracked ice, for serving

Wash and scrub the oysters well under cold running water to remove grit and sand from the shell.

To open an oyster: Put a thick glove on your left hand (if right-handed) or use a folded kitchen towel to cushion the oyster and protect your hand. Hold the oyster firmly in your left hand, cup-side down, hinge toward you, and insert the tip of an oyster knife into the hinge. Twist and work the knife into the oyster, applying gentle pressure. As soon as the point of the knife penetrates the hinge, twist the blade to pop the shell open. Slide the knife along the inside of the top shell to sever the muscle attachment. Discard the top shell and wipe the knife blade if necessary to remove any bits of shell that adhere to it.

Cut under the oyster meat to sever the bottom muscle attachment, being careful to conserve as much oyster liquor as possible.

Put the oyster on its half shell atop a bed of cracked ice to keep it cold. Proceed in the same manner until all the oysters are open. Oysters should be served as soon as possible after opening, preferably within 15 minutes.

ASSEMBLY: Line 4 dinner plates with cracked ice. Place 6 oysters on the half shell on each plate. Make sure the oysters are balanced and steady so they won't tip over before you serve them. You don't want to lose any of the liquor around the oyster. Just before serving, spoon some raspberry mignonette over each oyster or else put the vinaigrette in a ramekin and serve it on the side.

RASPBERRY MIGNONETTE
Calories 10; Protein 0 g/0 cal; Carbohydrates 3 g/10 cal;
Fat 0 g/0 cal; (Saturated Fat 0 g/0 cal); Cholesterol 0 mg;
Sodium 2 mg; Fiber 0 g; Vitamin A 3% of Daily Value

OYSTERS
Calories 67; Protein 8 g/32 cal; Carbohydrates 4 g/17 cal;
Fat 2 g/18 cal; (Saturated Fat .4 g/4 cal); Cholesterol 43 mg;
Sodium 90 mg; Fiber 0 g; Iron 24% of Daily Value

You can substitute sherry, balsamic, or red wine vinegar for raspberry. The shallots sweeten the vinegar. Mignonette is a French term for coarsely ground white pepper.

Oysters are good grilled or oven-roasted and seasoned with a bit of cream and black pepper. I also like them topped with steamed, julienned spinach and a bit of garlic butter.

When you are shopping for oysters, be careful to buy from reliable sources. Oysters vary in taste and shape. In the cold northeast, oysters are round, flat and somewhat salty. In the Chesapeake Bay, they are cupped, sweet and milky.

The Bay was once famous for its oysters, but ravaged by pollution and disease, they are down to a small percentage of their original population. Oysters are ecologically important. They are filter-feeders and an increased population can help create a healthy environment where sea grasses can prosper and water birds can thus find sites for nests.

WARM FRISÉE, RADICCHIO, AND BACON SALAD WITH GARLIC-THYME VINAIGRETTE

The French introduced me to salads with hot dressings. I love the French classic of mesclun or baby lettuces topped with hot sautéed chicken livers, and seasoned with a splash of raspberry vinaigrette.

If you prefer to avoid bacon fat, pour it all off after sautéing the garlic and bacon. Add 2 tablespoons of olive oil to the pan to use as the dressing's base.

Older and tougher frisée and radicchio are well suited to this salad and its hot, slightly sweet and sour dressing.

4 ounces frisée, washed and spun dry
8 ounces radicchio, washed and spun dry
4 ounces bacon, thinly sliced and cut into
  1-inch pieces
12 small garlic cloves, thinly sliced

1 tablespoon water
1 tablespoon red wine vinegar
1 tablespoon thyme leaves
Sea salt and freshly ground black pepper

Tear the frisée and radicchio into bite-size pieces and put them into a medium bowl.

Sauté the bacon over medium heat for 3 – 4 minutes to render some fat. Add the garlic and sauté for about 2 more minutes, stirring frequently, until the garlic is golden and the bacon is crisp. Remove the bacon and garlic with a slotted spoon and drain on paper towels. Pour off some of the bacon fat, leaving about 4 tablespoons in the sauté pan.

Add the water, vinegar, and thyme to the sauté pan and season to taste with salt and pepper. Use the salt sparingly—bacon is already salty. Bring the dressing to a boil and pour over the lettuces. Toss to combine.

ASSEMBLY: Divide the salad among 4 warm salad plates and garnish with bacon and garlic.

FRISÉE, RADICCIO, AND BACON SALAD
WITH DRESSING
Calories 65;   Protein 4 g/17 cal;   Carbohydrates 5 g/18 cal;
Fat 3 g/30 cal;   (Saturated Fat 1 g/10 cal);   Cholesterol 5 mg;
Sodium 129 mg;   Fiber 1 g;   Vitamin C 35% of Daily Value

CHICKEN AND CASHEW CURRY WITH BASMATI RICE, BROCCOLI, CHUTNEY, AND MINT RAITA

CHICKEN AND CASHEW CURRY ✳

Curry powder should have a complex flavor and requires many spices. I often doctor curry powder to suit my needs. For yogurt-based curry, I add more cardamom and ground coriander. For tomato-based curry, I add more cumin seeds and turmeric.

Garam masala is an Indian spice mixture added at the end of cooking to mellow the flavors. It contains cinnamon, cloves, nutmeg, cardamom, and black pepper. To make 1 cup garam masala, grind in a blender: 25 cardamom pods, seeds only, ¹/₂ cup black peppercorns, ¹/₂ cup cumin seeds, two 3-inch cinnamon sticks, 4–6 whole cloves, ¹/₂ cup coriander seeds, 1 tablespoon ground mace, and 6–8 bay leaves. If you want to reduce the heat, decrease the amount of black pepper.

Curries are some of my customers' favorite dishes. Good thing, because we always have a need to use the stew meat from our organic animals. I love making simmered dishes in the winter. They fill the whole house with aromatic, warm smells with homey appeal. I learned to make curries by reading Julie Sahni's books on Indian cooking.

4-inch piece of ginger, peeled and sliced across the grain
2 whole jalapeño or serrano chilies, stemmed
1 cup chicken stock or water
3 tablespoons canola oil
1¹/₂ pounds onions, minced, about 2 large onions
2 tablespoons minced garlic
3 tablespoons good quality curry powder, available at specialty stores
1 cup low-fat yogurt
Sea salt and freshly ground black pepper
6 chicken legs, about 2 pounds, skinned, boned, and cut into 1-inch pieces
2 teaspoons garam masala, available at specialty stores
1 tablespoon lemon juice
¹/₂ cup chopped cilantro
1 cup cashews

Put the ginger, chilies, and stock or water in a blender and purée until smooth.

Heat 2 tablespoons of the oil in a sauté pan or casserole large enough to hold all the ingredients. Sauté onions over low heat, stirring frequently for 20–30 minutes, until they are soft and golden. Add the garlic and the curry powder, and stir and sauté for about 2 more minutes. Add the chili-ginger mixture and yogurt and season to taste with salt and pepper. This is the base for your curry.

Heat the remaining oil in a sauté pan large enough to hold the chicken pieces in one layer, or else use a smaller pan and cook the chicken in batches. Sauté the chicken pieces for 3 minutes on each side or until they are browned.

Preheat the oven to 350° F.

Add the browned chicken to the curry base and stir to combine. Bring to a boil, reduce the heat, and simmer for 15–20 minutes, until chicken is tender.

Put the cashews on a baking sheet and roast them in the oven for about 10 minutes, until golden and toasted. You don't have to stir them.

Just before serving the curry, add the garam masala, lemon juice, cilantro, and cashews. Stir to combine and heat through for another 5 minutes.

3 cups of water

2 cups of basmati rice, available at health or specialty stores or other long grain rice

½ teaspoon sea salt

Grated peel of 1 lemon

Bring 3 cups of water to a boil in a medium saucepan. Add the rice, salt, and lemon peel. Return to a boil and, stirring to combine, lower the heat and cover. Simmer over a very low flame for about 14 minutes, until the rice is tender.

Uncover and stir with a fork to plump the rice and separate the grains.

BROCCOLI

½ pound broccoli florets

Steam the broccoli in a small saucepan using a collapsible steamer or cook it briefly in boiling water until tender, 3 – 5 minutes.

Broccoli is a cruciferous vegetable from the Mediterranean, high in Vitamin C and beta carotene. Broccoli tastes as good with scrambled eggs as it does with braised dishes. It works well in stir-fries and pastas. At Nora's, we serve the broccoli florets and use stems to make broccoli-ginger or broccoli-apple soup.

An easy way to grate a peeled cucumber is to hold it vertically, turning it as you grate the outer flesh, leaving the seedy core intact. A small grated onion also tastes good in raita.

Raita means yogurt salad in India and is often served with curries as a cooling accompaniment. In India, raitas are made with water buffalo milk which is thicker than cow's milk.

½ cup low-fat yogurt, drained if possible
½ cucumber, peeled and coarsely grated
2 pinches ground cumin

1 tablespoon chopped cilantro or mint
Sea salt and freshly ground black pepper

If you have time, put the yogurt in a colander lined with cheesecloth and drain it in the refrigerator for one hour, preferably more. (When mixed with the cucumber, such yogurt will produce a thicker, less watery raita.) Squeeze the grated cucumber very well between your fingers to drain it. This prevents the raita from becoming too liquid. Mix the cucumber with the yogurt, cumin, cilantro or mint. Season to taste with salt and pepper.

1 medium onion, chopped,

1-inch piece ginger, peeled and minced

2 cups dried apricots, about ³/₄ pound,
  preferably unsulphured, sliced in half
  or into ¹/₂-inch pieces

¹/₂ cup white or brown sugar

1 cup apple cider or rice wine vinegar

3 cups water

1 teaspoon curry powder

4 cardamom seed pods

One 2-inch cinnamon stick

Put the onion, ginger, apricots, sugar, vinegar, water, curry powder, cardamom, and cinnamon in a medium saucepan. Bring to a boil, reduce the heat, and simmer for 1 – 1¹/₂ hours, until the chutney takes on the consistency of a jam. Stir the chutney from time to time to prevent it from burning. Let cool.

If you want a spicy chutney, add some minced chili pepper to the mixture.

ASSEMBLY: Spoon some curry onto each of 4 warm dinner plates. Place a large spoonful of rice in the center of each plate. You can also press the rice into a 3- or 4-inch ramekin until it takes the dish's shape, then turn one of these onto each plate. Arrange some of the broccoli florets around the rice. Serve with chutney and cucumber raita on the side.

CHICKEN AND CASHEW CURRY

Calories 695;   Protein 44 g/176 cal;   Carbohydrates 45 g/180 cal;
Fat 38 g/340 cal;   (Saturated Fat 7 g/59 cal);   Cholesterol 107 mg;
Sodium 399 mg;   Fiber 5 g;   Iron 91% of Daily Value
You will significantly lower the fat in this recipe by using fewer cashews.

BROCCOLI

Calories 21;   Protein 2 g/7 cal;   Carbohydrates 3 g/12 cal;
Fat .2 g/2 cal;   (Saturated Fat 0 g/0 cal);   Cholesterol 0 mg;
Sodium 15 mg;   Fiber 1 g;   Vitamin C 87% of Daily Value

APRICOT CHUTNEY

Calories 33;   Protein .5 g/2 cal;   Carbohydrates 7 g/29 cal;
Fat .2 g/2 cal;   (Saturated Fat 0 g/0 cal);   Cholesterol 0 mg;
Sodium 2 mg;   Fiber 1 g;   Vitamin A 6% of Daily Value

BASMATI RICE

Calories 344;   Protein 7 g/29 cal;   Carbohydrates 73 g/292 cal;
Fat 3 g/23 cal;   (Saturated Fat 1 g/5 cal);   Cholesterol 0 mg;
Sodium 276 mg;   Fiber 2 g;   Iron 9% of Daily Value

MINT RAITA

Calories 29;   Protein 2 g/9 cal;   Carbohydrates 5 g/18 cal;
Fat .2 g/2 cal;   (Saturated Fat 0 g/0 cal);   Cholesterol 1 mg;
Sodium 22 mg;   Fiber 1 g;   Vitamin C 20% of Daily Value

Chutneys are relishes. Cooked chutneys are mostly made with pulpy fruits that are chopped and cooked with sugar, vinegar, and spices until they become a sweetish-sour jam.

I use chutneys with grilled mushrooms, fish, or chicken, and with rounds of goat cheese or grilled polenta. I also combine them with low-fat ricotta or goat cheese and serve them on toasted bread.

Store chutneys in a covered glass or plastic container in the refrigerator. They will keep for several weeks.

Bittersweet Chocolate Mousse with Caramel Sauce and Lemon Balm

Caramel Sauce ✳

Making caramel takes longer than you would imagine. Be patient and careful, and you will create a delicious sauce.

Caramel sauce can be made creamy by adding 2 tablespoons of heavy cream to the sugar syrup. It can also be made into a butterscotch sauce by adding 1 – 2 tablespoons butter and heavy cream and 1 shot of Scotch.

½ cup sugar

1 cup hot water

Heat the sugar in a small sauté pan on medium low heat until it starts to melt and turns a dark amber color, 5 – 7 minutes.

Add the hot water carefully; it can spatter because the sugar is so hot. Bring to a boil and cook, stirring with a metal spoon, until the caramel dissolves and the sauce is syrupy.

Remove the sauce from the heat. It will thicken as it cools.

Bittersweet Chocolate Mousse ✳

Refrigerate the mousse overnight, if possible

8 ounces good quality bittersweet chocolate, roughly chopped
1 cup heavy cream

2 tablespoons Kahlúa or Grand Marnier
7 – 8 egg whites
2 tablespoons confectioners' sugar
Fresh lemon balm for garnish

I love chocolate mousse and have always been annoyed that it is so high in calories and cholesterol. To reduce the cholesterol, I omit the egg yolks—if you use high-quality chocolate, you don't need them. This yolk-free mousse is not as firm as one made with whole eggs, but it tastes just as good.

I also use this mousse as a pastry filling and a cake frosting. Sometimes I serve it frozen. To do this, mold the mousse in a plastic-lined loaf pan and freeze, then cut into slices and allow to soften a bit before serving.

Melt the chocolate with the Kahlúa and 4 tablespoons of the cream in a double boiler over simmering water, stirring to combine. Remove from the heat and allow to cool.

Whip the egg whites until soft peaks form, add the confectioners' sugar, and whip for 1 more minute or until peaks are firm. Whip the remaining cream until it forms soft peaks.

Use a rubber spatula to gently stir the cooled melted chocolate into the beaten egg whites. Fold in the whipped cream, and incorporate well. Refrigerate for 2 hours or overnight, if possible. If in a hurry, freeze for 30 minutes to set the mousse.

ASSEMBLY: Pour some caramel sauce on 4 large plates and top with 3 small scoops of chocolate mousse. Garnish with a sprig of lemon balm.

CARAMEL SAUCE
Calories 96;   Protein 0 g/0 cal;   Carbohydrates 24 g/96 cal;
Fat 0 g/0 cal;   (Saturated Fat 0 g/0 cal);   Cholesterol 0 mg;
Sodium 2 mg;   Fiber 0 g

BITTERSWEET CHOCOLATE MOUSSE (6 OUNCES)
Calories 85;   Protein 2 g/8 cal;   Carbohydrates 3 g/12 cal;
Fat 7 g/63 cal;   (Saturated Fat 2 g/21 cal);   Cholesterol 12 mg;
Sodium 20 mg;   Fiber 1 g;   Vitamin A 12.4% of Daily Value

WINTER MENU IV

GRILLED LAMB KIDNEYS WITH MUSTARD DRESSING AND KALE

SEA SCALLOPS IN BLACK SESAME CRUST WITH ORANGE-GINGER SAUCE, CILANTRO SPAGHETTINI,
BROCCOLI, AND BUTTERNUT SQUASH

JULIENNE OF BELGIAN ENDIVE, SPINACH, AND RADICCHIO SALAD WITH MUSTARD VINAIGRETTE

CARAMELIZED BANANAS WITH LIME-TEQUILA ICE CREAM AND CHOCOLATE SAUCE

WINE SELECTIONS

Sea scallops have a delicate flavor. With the orange-ginger sauce, they are a perfect match to a crisp, dry Chenin Blanc.

Pine Ridge 1991 Napa Valley

Vouvray 1989 Gaston Huet

GRILLED LAMB KIDNEYS
WITH MUSTARD DRESSING* AND KALE

2 tablespoons tamari
1 tablespoon balsamic vinegar
3 tablespoons water
1 tablespoon Dijon mustard
½ cup of olive oil
½ teaspoon chopped garlic
1 teaspoon chopped thyme or flat leaf parsley

Freshly ground black pepper

12 lamb kidneys
2 teaspoons olive oil
½ pound of kale or other greens, washed and
    stemmed

Pour the tamari, vinegar, water, mustard, 7 tablespoons of the oil, garlic, and thyme or parsley into a blender. Purée until emulsified. Season to taste with pepper only—both tamari and mustard are salty. Reserve ¼ cup of the dressing for the Belgian endive salad (page 185).

Wash the kidneys and remove the outer membrane, if necessary. Cut them horizontally, ¾ of the way through, and open until they lie flat like the pages of a book. Use a small paring knife or curved sharp scissors to cut out the white fat at the center. The kidneys will have a small, donut shape with a hole at the center where the fat was removed.

Preheat the grill or broiler.

Brush the kidneys with 1 teaspoon of the remaining oil and season to taste with salt and pepper. Grill the kidneys for about 2 minutes on each side. They should still be pink inside because overcooked kidneys are very tough.

Blanch the kale or other greens in boiling water for 2 – 3 minutes or steam them in a medium saucepan using a collapsible steamer for 2 – 3 minutes or until bright green. Toss the greens with the remaining olive oil and season to taste with salt and pepper.

ASSEMBLY: Pour some mustard dressing in a pool on the side of each of 4 warm dinner plates. Arrange the kidneys in a semicircle on the side of the sauce. Garnish with the kale.

MUSTARD DRESSING
Calories 260; Protein 2 g/6 cal; Carbohydrates 4 g/14 cal;
Fat 27 g/240 cal; (Saturated Fat 4 g/35 cal); Cholesterol 0 mg;
Sodium 594 mg; Fiber 1 g; Vitamin C 8% of Daily Value

GRILLED LAMB KIDNEYS
Calories 290; Protein 23 g/92 cal; Carbohydrates 7 g/28 cal;
Fat 19 g/171 cal; (Saturated Fat 2 g/18 cal); Cholesterol 480 mg;
Sodium 730 mg; Fiber 0 g; Vitamin C 120% of Daily Value
Vitamin A 40% of Daily Value

Since we buy whole organic animals, we always have some type of organ meat on the menu at Nora's. Unfortunately, most Americans don't seem to appreciate innards. except for the small percentage that likes chicken and beef livers.

Organ meats are high in cholesterol, but they are also high in phosphorus, iron, potassium, and vitamins A and B. You should eat organ meats from organic animals only, since organs are the filters for the blood and retain any chemicals added to the feed.

Use this same recipe to prepare other kidneys or livers, but be careful to adjust the grilling time so you don't overcook them.

After we blanch our vegetables, we drain and toss them in a seasoned "bath" of olive oil, garlic, shallots, and salt and pepper.

Sea Scallops in Black Sesame Crust with Orange-Ginger Sauce, Cilantro Spaghettini, Broccoli, and Butternut Squash

ORANGE-GINGER SAUCE ✳

It is important to cool the orange juice before using it because the sauce will not thicken properly if made with warm juice.

You can serve this orange sauce with steamed spring rolls, sushi rolls, or gravlax rolls. I also serve it with an Asian-style grilled salmon with shiitakes, steamed baby bok choy, and crispy noodles.

Like all of the sauces I make in the blender, this orange-ginger sauce is emulsified. Be careful when reheating any emulsified sauce as it will break down if brought to a boil. Use low heat only. At Nora's, I keep the sauces at room temperature and ladle them onto hot plates just before serving.

3 shallots or one 2-inch piece of carrot
3 tablespoons canola oil
1 1/2 cups orange juice
2-inch piece ginger, peeled and sliced across the grain

Pinch saffron or turmeric
1 tablespoon rice wine vinegar or 1 teaspoon lemon juice
Sea salt and freshly ground black pepper

Preheat the oven to 400° F.

Put the shallots or carrot in a small baking dish with 1 teaspoon oil, cover with foil, and roast 30 – 40 minutes, until soft.

Pour the orange juice into a saucepan and boil until reduced by half. Remove from heat and cool to room temperature.

Put the orange juice, shallots or carrot, ginger, saffron or turmeric, and vinegar or lemon juice into a blender. Purée until smooth. Add the remaining oil in a thin stream as the motor runs. Blend until the sauce is smooth and shiny. Season to taste with salt and pepper.

STEAMED BUTTERNUT SQUASH OR CARROTS

1 pound butternut squash, peeled and seeded or
1/2 pound carrots, peeled and trimmed

Cut the squash or carrots into 1/2-inch cubes and steam in a medium saucepan using a collapsible steamer for 5 – 7 minutes until tender.

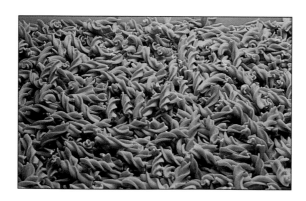

CILANTRO SPAGHETTINI

Pasta recipe (page 99)
4 tablespoons minced cilantro or flat leaf parsley

Make the pasta as described on page 99, substituting cilantro or parsley for saffron. Cut the pasta as thinly as possible, into spaghettini or spaghetti noodles.

1¼ — 1½ *pounds sea scallops*
2 *tablespoons black sesame seeds*
Sea salt and freshly ground black pepper
2 *tablespoons canola oil*

1 *pound broccoli, cut into small florets, stems removed*
Cilantro spaghettini
2 *ounces spinach, stemmed and washed*
Steamed butternut squash

Remove the tough muscle attachment from the sides of the scallops. Rinse briefly, drain, and dry on paper towels. Season to taste with salt and pepper. Pour the sesame seeds onto a salad plate and dip one side of each scallop in the seeds.

Heat 1 tablespoon canola oil in a medium sauté pan until hot. Put the scallops into the pan, sesame seeds down, and sauté them for 3 minutes or until the crust is slightly crisp.

Turn the scallops and brown the other side for 3 minutes or until the scallops are nearly cooked through and opaque. Remove the scallops from the sauté pan, drain them on a paper towel-lined dish, and cover with foil to keep warm.

Bring 6 — 8 quarts of water to a boil. Add the broccoli florets and cook for about 1 minute. Add the pasta and cook for another 2 — 3 minutes. Finally, add the spinach and cook one minute or until the spaghettini is al dente and the vegetables are bright green. Drain the vegetables and pasta in a colander, transfer them to a warm bowl, and add the steamed butternut squash and the remaining oil. Toss to combine. Season to taste with salt and pepper.

ASSEMBLY: Pour some orange-ginger vinaigrette on each of 4 warm dinner plates and tilt the plates to spread it evenly over the entire base. Divide the pasta among the 4 plates, placing it in the center. Arrange the scallops around the edge of the pasta.

ORANGE-GINGER SAUCE
Calories 144;   Protein 1 g/4 cal,   Carbohydrates 13 g/50 cal;
Fat 10 g/90 cal;   (Saturated Fat .8 g/7 cal);   Cholesterol 0 mg;
Sodium 3 mg;   Fiber 1 g;   Vitamin A 11% of Daily Value

CILANTRO SPAGHETTINI
Calories 171;   Protein 7 g/27 cal;   Carbohydrates 30 g/118 cal;
Fat 3 g/25 cal;   (Saturated Fat .7 g/6 cal);   Cholesterol 80 mg;
Sodium 157 mg;   Fiber 0 g;   Iron 14% of Daily Value

STEAMED BUTTERNUT SQUASH
Calories 48;   Protein 2 g/7 cal;   Carbohydrates 10 g/40 cal;
Fat .1 g/1 cal;   (Saturated Fat 0 g/0 cal);   Cholesterol 0 mg;
Sodium 5 mg;   Fiber 2 g;   Vitamin A 79% of Daily Value

SEA SCALLOPS IN A BLACK SESAME CRUST
Calories 226;   Protein 28 g/111 cal;   Carbohydrates 3 g/12 cal;
Fat 11 g/103 cal;   (Saturated Fat 1 g/9 cal);   Cholesterol 60 mg;
Sodium 302 mg;   Fiber 1 g;   Iron 20% of Daily Value

Julienne of Belgian Endive, Spinach, and Radicchio Salad with Mustard Vinaigrette

2 heads Belgian endive
½ pound spinach, washed, stemmed, and
    spun dry

1 head radicchio (4 – 6 ounces)
¼ cup mustard vinaigrette set aside from the
    kidney course

Wipe the endive clean with a damp cloth. Cut off the root end and separate into leaves. Stack the leaves and cut them lengthwise into julienne. Follow the same procedure for the radicchio and spinach.

ASSEMBLY: Combine the lettuces and toss with mustard vinaigrette. Arrange on each of 4 dinner plates.

BELGIAN ENDIVE, SPINACH AND RADICCHIO SALAD
Calories 23;   Protein 2 g/10 cal;   Carbohydrates 3 g/11 cal;
Fat .2 g/2 cal;   (Saturated Fat 0 g/0 cal);   Cholesterol 0 mg;
Sodium 53 mg;   Fiber 2 g;   Calcium 9% of Daily Value

Belgian endive and radicchio are bitter greens. Spinach is sweet and mustard is spicy. Combining these tastes makes for good balance in a salad, where the taste of each ingredient provides lively contrast for the others.

You can make this salad into a light meal by adding goat cheese, Brie, or Stilton, fruit, such as apple, pear, or grapes, and nuts, such as walnuts, pecans, or almonds.

Caramelized Bananas with Lime-Tequila Ice Cream and Chocolate Sauce

LIME-TEQUILA ICE CREAM *

I use the vanilla ice cream recipe as a base for nearly all the ice creams I make. I adapt the recipe by reducing or omitting the vanilla and substituting other flavorings. Be careful to avoid adding too much sugar or alcohol to the base or it will not freeze. And add enough sugar to give the ice cream a smooth texture. When working with a sweet ingredient such as maple syrup, reduce the sugar by one-half. For alcohol, a good rule is to add no more than ¹/₂ tablespoon per serving.

You will need an ice cream maker.
Vanilla ice cream (page 61)

6 tablespoons lime juice, juice from 3 – 4 limes
2 tablespoons Tequila

Follow the directions for making vanilla ice cream on page 61, but omit the vanilla flavoring, adding lime juice and tequila instead. Freeze in an ice cream maker following manufacturer's directions.

CHOCOLATE SAUCE ✳

6 ounces good quality, semi-sweet chocolate
6 tablespoons milk or heavy cream

2 tablespoons Kahlúa or other chocolate liqueur
(optional)

Put the chocolate, milk or cream, and Kahlúa in a double boiler and place it over simmering water to melt the chocolate. Stir to combine. The sauce will thicken as it cools.

This is an easy, all-purpose chocolate sauce. I use it for ice cream, sorbets, poached pears, and pound cake. For a richer version of the chocolate sauce, use heavy cream instead of milk.

CARAMELIZED BANANAS

4 tablespoons unsalted butter
4 tablespoons brown sugar
2 tablespoons tequila

4 bananas, peeled and cut into halves lengthwise
Zest of 1 lime for garnish
Fresh mint sprigs for garnish

Preheat the broiler.

Make a glaze by putting the butter, brown sugar, and tequila in a small sauté pan and heating it until it melts, stirring to blend.

Place the banana halves, cut-side-down, on a sheet pan. Pour the glaze over the bananas and broil them until the sugar bubbles and the bananas are lightly browned.

ASSEMBLY: Place 2 banana halves on each of 4 dinner plates. Spoon some of the glaze over them. Put a large scoop of the lime-tequila ice cream in the center. Drizzle some chocolate sauce over the bananas and the ice cream. Garnish with the lime zest and mint.

If you get this dessert right, the chocolate sauce hardens on the bananas like a banana Eskimo Pie.

This is high-calorie comfort food. You can also prepare the bananas in a large sauté pan. Melt the butter, add the sugar and tequila and then the bananas. Cook them until just tender being careful not to let them get too soft or they will fall apart when you transfer them to the serving dishes. These bananas are great even without the ice cream.

LIME–TEQUILA ICE CREAM (1 OUNCE)
Calories 81;   Protein 1 g/3 cal;   Carbohydrates 3 g/13 cal;
Fat 7 g/65 cal;   (Saturated Fat 4 g/39 cal);   Cholesterol 41 mg;
Sodium 8 mg;   Fiber 0 g;   Vitamin A 10% of Daily Value

CHOCOLATE SAUCE
Calories 105;   Protein 1 g/4 cal;   Carbohydrates 11 g/44 cal;
Fat 6 g/57 cal; (Saturated Fat 4 g/34 cal);   Cholesterol 1 mg;
Sodium 5 mg;   Fiber 1 g;   Iron 2% of Daily Value

CARAMELIZED BANANAS
Calories 249;   Protein 1 g/5 cal;   Carbohydrates 34 g/138 cal;
Fat 12 g/106 cal;   (Saturated Fat 7 g/66 cal);   Cholesterol 31 mg;
Sodium 90 mg;   Fiber 2 g;   Vitamin C 16% of Daily Value

WINTER MENU V

SPICED SHRIMP STEAMED IN OLD DOMINION BEER

BABY ROMAINE CAESAR SALAD WITH GARLIC CROUTONS, FARM EGGS, AND PARMESAN

ROASTED DUCK LEGS AND WINTER VEGETABLES

LEMON POPPY SEED CAKE WITH WARM PRUNE-PORT COMPOTE

WINE SELECTIONS

A soft, full-bodied red Chianti Classico from Italy is needed to stand up to the rich flavor of duck.

Chianti Rampolla 1985 Italy

Chianti Monsanto 1985 Italy

SPICED SHRIMP STEAMED IN OLD DOMINION BEER

1 ½ cups Old Dominion or a pilsner-type
  beer
1 teaspoon Old Bay seasoning, available in
  specialty stores, or a mixture of celery
  salt, pepper, paprika, mace, ginger, bay
  leaves, and cloves

1 ¼ pound large shrimp, peeled and deveined
Small bouquet of flat leaf parsley for garnish

Pour the beer and Old Bay seasoning into a medium saucepan, stir to combine, and simmer for 5 minutes. Add the shrimp, stir, and bring back to a boil. Remove the saucepan from the heat, cover, and leave for 3 minutes until the shrimp are opaque and cooked through. If you won't be serving the shrimp immediately, transfer them from the hot pan into a bowl so they don't continue cooking. Shrimp grow tough when overcooked.

ASSEMBLY: Divide the shrimp among 4 large, warm soup bowls and pour some broth into each bowl. Garnish each bowl with a small bunch of parsley.

SPICED SHRIMP
Calories 149;   Protein 30 g/120 cal;   Carbohydrates 4 g/15 cal;
Fat 2 g/14 cal;   (Saturated Fat .4 g/4 cal);   Cholesterol 275 mg;
Sodium 323 mg;   Fiber 1 g;   Iron 27% of Daily Value

When I cook this dish at home, I leave the shells on the shrimp, and use 1 tablespoon of Old Bay. Then everyone peels their own shrimp as we sit around the table and talk. Most commercially available shrimp and scallops are sprayed with a preservative. At Nora's, we buy our shrimp and scallops from companies who do not use this spray. I don't think it is safe to eat food with preservatives and chemical additives. No one knows how these chemicals may change and damage the body.

Old Bay seasoning or "crab boil" is a traditional spice mixture from the Chesapeake Bay area used to season hard-shell crabs. It is quite salty and spicy and can overwhelm a dish when too much is added, so be careful to use sparingly.

Baby Romaine Caesar Salad with Garlic Croutons, Farm Eggs, and Parmesan

CAESAR DRESSING

2 teaspoons minced garlic
2 anchovy fillets
1 tablespoon Worcestershire sauce
2 teaspoons Dijon mustard
1 tablespoon grated Parmesan cheese
$\frac{1}{4}$ cup water
1 tablespoon lemon juice
Freshly ground black pepper
$\frac{1}{2}$ cup olive oil

Put the garlic, anchovies, Worcestershire sauce, mustard, Parmesan, water, lemon juice, and pepper to taste in a blender. Blend until smooth. While the motor is running, slowly pour the oil into the blender in a thin stream and blend until emulsified. Taste and adjust for seasoning.

GARLIC CROUTONS

1 teaspoon minced garlic
1 tablespoon olive oil
Sea salt and freshly ground black pepper
$\frac{1}{3}$ loaf French or Italian country bread, cut into $\frac{1}{2}$-inch cubes

Preheat the oven to 450° F.

Mix the garlic, olive oil, salt, and pepper in a medium bowl. Add the bread cubes and toss with the seasoning. Spread the cubes onto a baking sheet and bake for 12 – 15 minutes, stirring once or twice, or until the croutons are lightly browned and crunchy. Remove from the oven and cool.

BABY ROMAINE CAESAR SALAD

4 heads baby romaine lettuce ($\frac{1}{2}$ pound)
3 eggs
4 – 6 ounce wedge of Parmesan cheese
Garlic croutons
Caesar dressing

Fill a saucepan with 2 or 3 cups of water and bring to a boil. Carefully add the eggs so they do not crack, reduce the heat, and simmer for 4 – 6 minutes, until they are hard-boiled but the yolk is still moist. Remove the eggs from the saucepan, cool under running water, peel and quarter.

Trim the baby romaine, separate the leaves and wash and dry them.

ASSEMBLY: Toss the romaine lettuce with the Caesar dressing. Divide the greens among 4 dinner plates. Add 3 egg quarters to each plate and sprinkle each salad with croutons.

Use a vegetable peeler or cheese slicer to shave thin curls of Parmesan onto each salad, as a garnish.

CAESAR DRESSING

Calories 272;   Protein 3 g/10 cal;   Carbohydrates 2 g/7 cal;
Fat 28 g/255 cal;   (Saturated Fat 4 g/35 cal);   Cholesterol 5 mg;
Sodium 258 mg;   Fiber 0 g;   Calcium 5% of Daily Value

BABY ROMAINE CAESAR SALAD

Calories 158;   Protein 14 g/55 cal;   Carbohydrates 3 g/10 cal;
Fat 10 g/93 cal;   (Saturated Fat 1 g/8 cal);   Cholesterol 134 mg;
Sodium 432 mg;   Fiber 1 g;   Calcium 35% of Daily Value

GARLIC CROUTONS

Calories 107;   Protein 2 g/8 cal;   Carbohydrates 15 g/59 cal;
Fat 4 g/40 cal;   (Saturated Fat .7 g/6 cal);   Cholesterol 0 mg;
Sodium 150 mg;   Fiber 0 g;   Iron 4% of Daily Value

There is a remarkable difference between Parmigiano Reggiano and other Parmesan cheese. Parmigiano Reggiano is produced under strict standards, aged over one year, and officially inspected. It is delicious to eat with fresh fruit or in a fennel salad.

ROASTED DUCK LEGS AND WINTER VEGETABLES

If you are starting with a whole duck, use the breast first and freeze the legs and wings to use in this recipe because they are less affected by frost.

In the last ten years, Americans have begun to eat more duck. For many years, Peking and Long Island duck were the only kinds available. The domestic production of foie gras introduced Muscovy and Barbary ducks. I find Muscovy ducks leaner than Peking and the meat more flavorful.

This dish can be prepared with a small roast of pork, veal, lamb, or beef. Since lamb and beef are eaten medium rare, they need less time to cook than pork or veal, and the vegetables should be precooked or cut into a smaller dice.

4 duck legs, preferably Muscovy duck
4 duck wings, if reserved
2 large carrots, (¾ pound) peeled, cut into 1½-inch pieces
8 small new potatoes, (¾ pound)
8 baby turnips, trimmed and quartered
8 baby beets (½ pound) or parsnips, peeled, and quartered or sliced
4 ribs celery (½ pound), cut into 1½-inch pieces

4 shallots, peeled
4 whole garlic heads, with ⅓ of the top trimmed off to expose a cross-section of the cloves
4 teaspoons olive oil
4 tablespoons mixed chopped herbs, such as rosemary, thyme, oregano, and parsley
Sea salt and freshly ground black pepper
1 cup duck stock, chicken stock or white wine
Celery leaves, for garnish

Preheat the oven to 350° F.

Put the duck, carrots, potatoes, turnips, beets, celery, shallots, whole garlic heads, and 3 teaspoons oil into a large bowl. Season to taste with chopped herbs, salt, and pepper. Toss to combine. Oil a 9 x 14-inch roasting pan with the remaining oil. Remove the duck legs and wings from the bowl and place them into the baking dish.

Pour ½ cup stock or wine into the baking dish. Roast the duck for 30 minutes, turning once so it will brown evenly.

Add the seasoned vegetables and remaining stock or wine to the roasting pan with the duck. Roast for 45 minutes or until the duck and vegetables are browned and cooked through.

ASSEMBLY: Divide the vegetables among 4 warm plates, then place a duck leg and wing on each. Pour the accumulated juices over the meat and vegetables. Garnish with celery leaves.

ROASTED DUCK LEGS AND WINTER VEGETABLES
Calories 495;   Protein 29 g/115 cal;   Carbohydrates 36 g/144 cal;
Fat 15 g/136 cal;   (Saturated Fat 5 g/45 cal);   Cholesterol 89 mg;
Sodium 226 mg;   Fiber 7 g;   Iron 31% of Daily Value

LEMON POPPY SEED CAKE
WITH WARM PRUNE-PORT COMPOTE

Use a vegetable peeler to remove the skin from the lemon, being careful to avoid the bitter underlying pith. I never use peels from fruit that is not organically grown, because they are often sprayed with spoilage retardant, ripener, and food coloring. If you use non-organic fruit, please wash and scrub it thoroughly with warm water before removing the peel.

My friend, Shelley Getchell, told me a clever use for cloves. When you store empty glass jars, add a clove to each one and the closed jar will smell fresh and new when you open it again.

Gretchen Eiselt, one of my former chef's at Nora's, created this dessert. This pound cake, made with oil instead of butter, is a delicious example of how good low-cholesterol desserts can be.

We make several variations of this cake, seasoning them after baking by piercing them all over with a toothpick and pouring liquor over them. We make a rum-flavored lemon cake (omitting the poppy seeds). We also make an orange-Grand Marnier version.

PRUNE-PORT COMPOTE

1 1/2 cups ruby port
4 whole cloves
Peel from 1 lemon
2-inch piece of cinnamon stick
2 cardamom pods
1/2-inch piece of ginger, peeled and chopped
1/2 pound dried prunes, pitted
Mint for garnish

Pour the port into a medium, non-reactive saucepan and add the cloves, lemon peel, cinnamon, cardamom, and ginger. Bring to a boil. Add the dried prunes, reduce the heat, and simmer for 15 minutes or until the fruit is soft.

LEMON POPPY SEED CAKE ✳

1 tablespoon poppy seeds
4 eggs
1 1/3 cups sugar
3/4 cup canola oil
1 1/3 cup unbleached organic flour
1 1/3 teaspoons baking powder
1/3 teaspoon salt
1/3 cup milk
Grated peel of 2 lemons
Mint sprigs as garnish

Preheat oven to 325° F.

Toast the poppy seeds for 1 minute in a dry sauté pan, shaking and stirring the pan, so as not to burn the seeds. Allow to cool.

Put the eggs, sugar, and oil in the bowl of an electric mixer with a paddle attachment and mix until smooth, about 2 minutes. You can also mix by hand with a whip. Add the flour, baking powder, salt, and poppy seeds and mix for 1 more minute or until well combined.

Add the milk and lemon peel and mix one last minute. Scrape the sides and bottom of the mixing bowl to make sure the batter is thoroughly combined.

Oil an 8-inch springform pan. Pour the cake batter into the pan and bake for 50 minutes or until a toothpick inserted into the middle of the cake comes out clean. Let the cake sit in the pan for 10 minutes, then turn it out on a cake rack to finish cooling.

ASSEMBLY: Ladle some of the juice from the prune compote into each of 4 shallow dessert bowls. Cut 4 slices of poppy seed cake and put one slice just off center on each plate. Add 3 or 4 prunes to each plate and garnish with a sprig of mint. Serves 12.

PRUNE-PORT COMPOTE
Calories 242;   Protein 3 g/11 cal;   Carbohydrates 55 g/221 cal;
Fat 1 g/10 cal;   (Saturated Fat 0 g/0 cal);   Cholesterol 0 mg;
Sodium 23 mg;   Fiber 6 g;   Iron 15% of Daily Value

LEMON POPPY-SEED CAKE
Calories 339;   Protein 4 g/16 cal;   Carbohydrates 34 g/135 cal;
Fat 21 g/188 cal;   (Saturated Fat 2 g/18 cal);   Cholesterol 71 mg;
Sodium 119 mg;   Fiber 0 g;   Calcium 5% of Daily Value

WINTER MENU VI

Winter Vegetarian Plate

GRILLED EGGPLANT STEAK WITH ROASTED RED PEPPERS, FETA CHEESE, BLACK OLIVES, AND PITA BREAD

SHIITAKE, TAT SOI, AND LEEK TART WITH WATERCRESS

WINE SELECTIONS

Even without meat, this menu has some strong flavors. Black olives and feta cheese are exciting
tastes to match with wine. A good choice is a red Brunello di Montalcino from Italy.

Brunello di Montalcino Il Poggione 1985

Brunello di Montalcino Altesino 1985

GRILLED EGGPLANT STEAK WITH ROASTED RED PEPPERS, FETA CHEESE, BLACK OLIVES, AND PITA BREAD

1 large eggplant, about 1 pound
Tamari-balsamic marinade (page 81)
2 medium red peppers, roasted, peeled, and cut into ½-inch cubes
¼ pound feta cheese, cut into small cubes or crumbled
½ cup black olives, pitted, preferably Greek or Moroccan (optional)

2 tablespoons chopped fresh oregano or flat leaf parsley
Sea salt and freshly ground black pepper
4 small pita breads for garnish
4 teaspoons balsamic vinegar
Bouquet of fresh oregano for garnish

I prefer to grill eggplant—it absorbs so much oil when sautéed. Grilled eggplant tastes wonderful and can be used in many ways. Layer it like a lasagna with ricotta cheese and tomato sauce, on a sandwich with tomatoes and arugula, or use it as part of a ratatouille.

Preheat grill or broiler.

Grill or broil the peppers, turning them until all the skin blisters and chars. Put the peppers into a bowl, seal with some plastic wrap, and allow to steam for 6 – 8 minutes.

When the peppers are cool enough to handle, peel off the charred outer skin and seed them. Rinse the peppers quickly under running water, if necessary. Cut into ½-inch cubes.

Cut the eggplant lengthwise into ½-inch thick slices to resemble a steak. Brush the eggplant steaks with the balsamic-tamari marinade and grill or broil for 2 minutes on each side, until tender but not too soft.

Put the red peppers, feta, olives, and oregano in a small bowl and season to taste with salt and pepper. Add the leftover marinade and stir to combine.

Toast or grill the pita bread and cut it into wedges.

ASSEMBLY: Place an eggplant steak on each of 4 warmed dinner plates. Put 2 spoonfuls of the pepper, olive, and feta salad on top of the eggplant. Sprinkle with balsamic vinegar. Garnish with a small bouquet of fresh oregano and pita bread wedges.

GRILLED EGGPLANT STEAK WITH ROASTED
RED PEPPERS, FETA CHEESE, BLACK OLIVES,
AND PITA BREAD
Calories 227;   Protein 9 g/35 cal;   Carbohydrates 35 g/141 cal;
Fat 6 g/51 cal;   (Saturated Fat 3 g/27 cal);   Cholesterol 14 mg;
Sodium 410 mg;   Fiber 4 g;   Calcium 175 of Daily Value

Shiitake, Tat Soi, and Leek Tart with Watercress*

Savory pies or tarts are great for putting a fresh dress on left-overs. Any combination works: you just have to combine the vegetables with some form of custard to hold them together.

If you want to omit the cheese from your custard, increase the number of eggs to three.

You don't have to use shiitakes in this recipe. Try making it with criminis, oysters, chanterelles, or morels, or use a combination of the wild mushrooms, fresh or dried.

Pie crust, see the recipe on page 44 and substitute a pinch of salt for the sugar
1 tablespoon olive oil
2 tablespoons chopped shallots
1 tablespoon chopped garlic
2 leeks, washed and sliced, green parts included
½ pound shiitake mushrooms, cleaned and thinly sliced
4 ounces tat soi or spinach, washed and dried
¼ cup milk
1 egg beaten
3 ounces low-fat ricotta or diced goat cheese
2 tablespoons chopped fresh herbs such as sage, rosemary, parsley, and thyme
Sea salt and freshly ground black pepper
1 bunch watercress for garnish

Preheat the oven to 425° F.

Make the pie crust following the recipe on page 30. Another method of rolling out the dough and one which avoids using extra flour is layering the dough between two large pieces of plastic wrap. Roll it out to a thickness of ⅛ of an inch. Put the dough in the freezer for 10 minutes or in the refrigerator for 30 minutes, until the dough is very cold and the plastic wrap will peel off easily.

Line four 3-inch tart pans or one 8 – 9-inch tart pan with the pastry, shaping but not stretching it to fit. Trim the dough leaving a 1-inch border of dough. Fold this dough over to double the sides of the tart and crimp the edges. Prick the bottom of the tart shell all over with a fork to prevent it from puffing up in spots as it bakes.

Bake the unfilled pie shells for 12 minutes or until lightly browned. Check the shells or shell after 5 minutes to see if parts of it are puffing up. If so, gently push these spots down and continue baking. Check after another 5 minutes and repeat the process, if necessary. Remove the shells from the oven.

Heat the oil in a medium sauté pan, add the shallots, garlic, and leeks, and sauté for 3 – 4 minutes, until lightly browned. Add the mushrooms and tat soi and cook for an additional 2 – 3 minutes, until softened. Remove from the heat.

Pour the milk into a small bowl, add the egg, ricotta or goat cheese, and chopped herbs and whisk together. Season to taste with salt and pepper.

Add the custard mixture to the vegetables in the sauté pan. Stir to combine. Pour this mixture into the 4 small or 1 large pre-baked tart shells.

Reduce the oven to 375° F.

Bake small tarts for 10 – 15 minutes and a larger tart for 20 – 25 minutes, until the filling is nearly firm and lightly browned. Allow the tarts to cool and set for at least 10 minutes before removing them from the pans.

Assembly: If you are using tart pans with removable sides, slip them off. If not, cut the large tart into 4 portions. Place each tart portion on a dinner plate and garnish with a small bouquet of watercress.

SHIITAKE, TAT SOI AND LEEK TART WITH
WATERCRESS
Calories 138; Protein 6 g/25 cal; Carbohydrates 14 g/55 cal;
Fat 6 g/58 cal; (Saturated Fat 1 g/9 cal); Cholesterol 62 mg;
Sodium 57 mg; Fiber 3 g; Vitamin A 20% of Daily Value

FARMERS

STONEBRIDGE FARM — CATHERINE CONOVER, OWNER
Stonebridge Farm, a large property in Virginia, belongs to a good customer and now friend of Nora Poullion and Steven Damato. Catherine Conover believed so strongly in Restaurant Nora's commitment to organic ingredients that she sought a personal way to help the restaurant receive a larger selection and supply of organic vegetables. Now, every Wednesday, Stonebridge Farm's gardener, Austin, delivers his vegetables and his famous baby lettuces to Restaurant Nora and City Cafe.

POTOMAC VEGETABLE FARM — HIU AND HANA NEWCOMB, OWNERS
Nora's relationship with Potomac Farm dates back to 1976, when Hiu Newcomb first began organic farming. An early pioneer, Hiu was the only local farmer at that time to offer organic produce. Nora herself continues to drive to rural Virginia to buy their famous Oriental greens, such as tat soi, bok choy, and mizuna. These days, Hiu's daughter, Hana, oversees the farm's daily operation.

HUMMINGBIRD FARM — JENNIFER STURMER, OWNER
Seven years ago, Jennifer Sturmer started growing hydroponic tomatoes in a small greenhouse in rural Maryland. Today, she owns four enormous greenhouses, and business is thriving. During the winter months, when most tomatoes are pale and flavorless, Hummingbird Farm's red, tasty tomatoes are a blessing for Restaurant Nora and City Cafe.

WINKELMAN'S FARM — EUGENE WINKELMAN, OWNER
Eugene Winkelman's farm looks like Noah's ark—so many kinds of animals are represented, all allowed to roam freely. This seventy-year-old farmer of Swiss origin raises the veal for Restaurant Nora and City Cafe in the old-fashioned way. The male calves, bought from neighboring dairy farms, are nursed by his cows for ten to twelve weeks. The humane manner in which he raises his veal is much appreciated by concerned customers of Restaurant Nora and City Cafe.

C.C. COCHRAN FARM — CARTER COCHRAN, SR., OWNER
When Carter Cochran retired from the Department of Agriculture five years ago, he was a man in search of an outdoor activity. On a small wooded section on his property, he had a go at growing mushrooms. Today, Cochran has 4,000 logs that produce over thirty pounds of shiitakes a week for Restaurant Nora and

local farmers markets. With such an abundant source of top-quality, fresh mushrooms, shiitakes are featured daily on Restaurant Nora's menu in everything from roasted shiitake relish to lump crab-shiitake cakes.

FLICKERVILLE FARM – CASS PETERSON, OWNER

After long and highly-regarded careers at *The Washington Post*, Cass Peterson and her partner Ward Sinclair launched a successful organic farm in rural Pennsylvania. For five winters, Nora has met with Ward and Cass to choose which specialty vegetables Flickerville Farm will grow for the restaurant. This relationship has allowed Restaurant Nora's guests to enjoy an enormous variety of tomatoes, peppers, greens, and salads. During the growing season, Ward would arrive each Tuesday, personally escorting his bounty, including the ten varieties of tomato for which the farm has become famous. Sadly, we recently lost Ward to a sudden illness and now Cass is continuing at the farm, arriving at our door each week with the most beautiful produce that you can imagine!

GARNETT C.B.S. FARM – STEPHEN GARNETT, OWNER

The Garnett family was the first organic meat supplier to work with Nora. Since 1976, when Stephen's father Gwynn read of Nora's commitment to organic foods, the Garnetts have shared their beef with her. The animals, raised without growth hormones or antibiotics, are fed a homegrown mix of organic corn, alfalfa, and kelp-a diet which accounts for the superb flavor in popular dishes like beef carpaccio. Each week, Stephen brings to the restaurant his beef, along with lamb and veal from local farmers whom he advises about organic farming. Stephen has quite a relationship with his animals; when he appears in the pasture and utters a particular sound, they all come running.

THE FARM AT MOUNT WALDEN – RICHARD PLA-SILVA AND KYLE STROHMANN, OWNERS

When their small, hot-smoked trout business grew more quickly than they expected, former advertising executive Richard Pla-Silva and his partner, Kyle Strohmann, found it hard to keep up with demand. Originally, Pla-Silva and Strohmann bought local trout and applewood from farms in Mount Walden, Virginia, and sold their succulent smoked fish at local farmers markets. Word spread and orders came flying in. Today, the pair operate their own smokehouse in the Plains, Virginia and sell their moist, low-salt trout in their own shop, as well as to Nora. Without it, her celebrated dish of smoked trout and roasted new baby potato-green bean salad with fresh horseradish sauce wouldn't be the same

IN APPRECIATION

With so many people to thank, I will try to do it in an orderly way, without sounding like a windy award recipient. I am particularly grateful to the following people:

My Japanese agent and now friend, Hiromi Hayashi, who contacted me and convinced me that the Japanese people want and need my cookbook. Her husband, Koji Hayashi, who took these beautiful photographs. Kuniaki Takashi, the senior editor, who let me have the freedom to create my cookbook and who twice made the long journey from Japan.

Karen Thomas, who listened and corrected my prose again and again. Ken Cook, who put it in nice shape for the computer. Candy Sagon and Joanna Pruess for editing the manuscript. Ann Yonkers for testing the recipes with me and writing them down legibly. Alison Zaremba for reading and retesting the recipes. Lauren R. Braun, who accepted the challenge to do detailed nutrition information in record time. Nancy Nickerson for patiently teaching me to use the computer.

My partners, Steven and Thomas Damato, for their encouragement and support, and again to Steven for taking care of our daughter, Nina, so that I could concentrate on this book.

My dedicated chefs and kitchen staff in both restaurants for performing so well while I was working on this book. My friends Susan Sechler, Ann Sabloff, Mark Newville, Marston Luce, Liz Stevens, Bobby Ng, Carole Ridker, and Debbie Appler for lending me their china and linens for the photographs.

My friend Shelley Getchell who introduced me to French cooking. It was in her library that I discovered Elizabeth David and was hooked from then on. James Beard who, through his books, taught me about simple American food. His writings always inspire me.

My first husband, Pierre Pouillon, who encouraged me and appreciated my efforts to learn and was a very constructive critic. My sons, Alexis and Olivier Pouillon, for being so understanding when I opened the restaurant and worked day and night so there was little time for them. My daughter Nina Fiona Emanuela Damato for being so good and helpful. Isabelle Baba and Fifi Fall for being such great babysitters and playmates for Nina.

All of my students, customers, and friends—especially Sally Quinn and Ben Bradlee, Elizabeth and John Newhouse, Kristina Kiehl and Bob Friedman, and

David Schwarz—who believed in me, helped me realize my dreams, and supported me during the last 20 years.

And lastly, to my parents, Gertraude and Leopold Aschenbrenner, who introduced me to good, healthy food and living as a child.

ABOUT THE AUTHOR

Born in Vienna in 1943, Nora Pouillon spent her childhood in Austria. In 1965, she arrived in Washington, D.C. as a newlywed. Eight years later, with her two sons in school, Nora opened a catering company and cooking school in her home. By the time she started a restaurant in a small Washington hotel in 1976, Nora Pouillon was a firm believer in organic food and had begun to translate her concern for healthy eating and living into an innovative, fresh style of cooking. After two years, Nora and her partners, Steven and Thomas Damato, moved to their present location and opened Restaurant Nora. They opened a second restaurant in 1987 which became Asia Nora in 1994.

INDEX